Woman Of God: Who Did God Create You to Be?

Christy Sanderson

Copyright © 2016

By Christy Sanderson

All rights reserved. No part of this publication may be reproduced, stored in a retrieval system, or transmitted, in any form, or by any means, electronic, mechanical, photocopying, recording, or otherwise, without the prior consent of the publisher.

ISBN-13: 978-1523659623
ISBN-10: 1523659629

Dedication

This book is dedicated to my Heavenly Father God, my natural father, Edward Sanderson and my belated mother, Toni Warren Sanderson.

Woman Of God: Who Did God Create You To Be?

Christy Sanderson

Table of Contents

Introduction

Fear You Are Dead To Me

Suicide Thoughts

Have You Ever Felt Broken

Can I Trust You?

You Asked Me "Do I Love You?"

You Cannot Be GOD in A Person's Life

God Loves You: But Are You Ready For Love

Is Money Really The Root Of All Evil?

Overcoming Molestation

I Am the Woman Who God Created Me to Be

A Single Mother Cry

A Single Mother

Who Shall Separate You from the Love of God?

Trust Issues

I Saw My Angel

Sex Outside Of Marriage

My Husband Went Through God First

Spend Time with God

Know Your Worth

The Spirit of Poverty

The Spirit of Homosexuality

Stop Trying to Figure Out whether That Person is real or fake

Break Every Chain

Are You Ready To Say Yes to God?

The World Will Hate You

Sow a Seed

You're A Lost Child on the Inside

Keep Your Faith

Spiritual Battle

Jezebel's Spirit

The Fire of God

Kingdom Of God

What is Wealth?

Just Be Yourself

Traditions and Religious

Prayer and Fasting

What Is Your Purpose?

We Have Failed As Women in Society

Woman of God

About the Author

Introduction: Who Are You?

When people look at you, they can't figure you out, they know you are different. Who are you, where do you come from, why are you so beautiful? Why do you always have a smile on your face? It's a glow on you but you're not pregnant. You're so different but you're so special, words can't even describe you. People envy you but when you enter a room, the whole atmosphere changes. How do you keep yourself so well-groomed and fashionable dress? Who is this woman, what makes her so different from me? Her hair is so long and even, her lips are so beautiful, her nails are so pretty and her teeth are so white. When she speaks her words are wise and she speaks of wisdom. Her heart is pure; she loves and cares about people, even those who spread lies about her. Whatever she goes she lights up the rooms, little children love and adore her and even the teenagers admire her. But people don't know about her past or what she has been through they just see a pretty face.

This woman is Christy Sanderson and she is a woman of God. What makes her so different is that she stands out from everyone else and she did not follow the in crowd. She strives and lives for The Lord regardless of what the world thinks or says about her. This woman loves God with all her heart; she knows people are watching her so she brings people closer to Jesus Christ. Many people have doubted her but she refuses to give up because she knows it's so many people lost in this world just like she once was.

Why does she love people so much? Christy knows that we all are a part of Abraham's seed and God created all of us with a purpose. She goes out into the world to save all the lost souls and bring them closer to Christ. Her purpose in life is to bring people closer to Christ, live for The Lord and to help people to become financially free. How can she do that? Christy let God's will be done in her life, let God guide and lead the way for her. Many women may ask how I can become close to God like her. Her response is if you let me help you, I will show you how to be lead by the Holy Spirit; in fact, the Holy Spirit will guide you to the process so the glory of God will shine through you. In John 14:12 "Verily, verily, I say unto you, He that believeth on me, the works that I do shall he also do; and greater works than these shall he do; because I go unto my Father." In this verse, it states that whoever has faith will do the same things as Jesus Christ did but some may even do greater things if you simply believe.

I leave you with these questions; my questions for you are Who Are You? Who did God create you to be and what is your purpose in life? Are you fulfilling God's purpose or are you're following the crowd?

When I first start writing these different stories, I was at my lowest point in life. Then I realize everything I went through was to bring me closer to God. That's why I would get over all the hurt and pain, I would write whatever God put on my heart. My purpose of writing this book is to help others that went through some of the same things I went through. It is to help women to find their purpose in life and to become the woman God created them to be.

Fear You Are Dead To Me

Who are you? Where do you come from? You do not come from God but the enemy uses you to stop people from becoming the person God created them to be. I hate you, I can't stand you, you ruin so many of God's people lives. I bury you in the name of Jesus. I wrote you a note with your name written all over it, cut into pieces. You block people blessings, you hurt people, and you stop them from trusting God and stepping out on faith.

You are not a part of God; you are the enemy so you must die in the name of Jesus. I hate you, I dislike your ways, and you sneak up on people before they reach their breakthroughs. However, you fill their minds with doubts and disbeliefs. You discourage God's people; you caused them not to believe in themselves. You only come to steal, kill and destroy Godly people. You are a liar, a cheater, and a heart breaker. I won't allow you back into my life. You have used me and mistreated me for far too long. I've taken control of my life again.

But I'm not like most people, I conquer you and I refuse to let you take control of my life. You may have taken my family lives but you won't take mine. I walk with faith, integrity and I live in the atmosphere of God. I won't settle for anything less, I get tired of you taking control of Godly people lives.

That's why I sent you right back to Hell where you belong. You must die in the name of Jesus because you are dead to me. From this day forward I refuse to let you enter into my life. In fact, anything that is not like God is already dead to me. You might have taken others' lives but not mine. You only come to weak minded people but I have control of my mind. You oh sneaky bastard, you smile in people faces but you're so fake. I see that evil smile but just know I'm one step ahead of you. God has my back; he would not allow me to be consumed by you so that's why He tells me things ahead of time. You shall die by the precious blood of Jesus Christ.

Who are you again? Oh that's right you're nobody, you're nothing to me. You died a long time ago when I decided to step out on faith and follow the Holy Spirit. You've tried to stop me but my Heavenly Father had other plans for me.

Therefore by the power of the son, and Holy Ghost I cast you back into the lake of fire Fear! You are officially dead to me in the name of Jesus! In 2 Timothy 1:7 "For God has not given us the spirit of fear; but of power, and of love, and of a sound mind."

Men and women of God stop being afraid take your lives back and do not allow fear to take control of your lives. God will always work things out on your behalves but you must do your part first. You're the only person who can save yourselves from fear!

Suicide Thoughts

Are you having suicide thoughts? You're frustrated and it seems like everything is going wrong in your life. Your marriage is falling apart; you're tired of being lied to and cheated on. You have lost your job, your house, your car, and your finances are falling apart. Your kids are acting up in school; your family has turned against you. All of your friends have walked away from you and have turned their backs on you. You're depressed, you're stressed out about everything, you don't know where your next move is, and you don't know what to do. You're trying to figure out things on your own. You're wondering where did I go wrong, how can I turn this situation around.

You're tired of struggling and being a single mother, things are getting too hard. Everyone knows your situation but no one is willing to help you. You had a child out of wedlock so you can't forgive yourselves. People are laughing at you, talking about you behind your backs and calling you everything but your name.

You have turned to drugs or alcohol because it seems like you have no other way out. But that didn't work so you turn to men for attention but it's the wrong type of men. He is now selling your body in the streets; you are now dancing on strip poles. Now who do you turn too, there is no other way out so you tried to take your own life away. That failed and it didn't work because God saved your life at the very last minute.

Woman of God I'm here to tell you, you have been looking for happiness in all the wrong places; you have to search to Jesus Christ for answers. God is the only person who can save you. It doesn't matter what your life looks like or what you have done in your past, God has already forgiven you. God has a purpose for your life, so never think about taking your own life again.

This is personal to me because I tried to take my own life. At the end of the year of 2012, I was at the lowest point in my life. I had hit rock bottom, my son's father had walked out our lives at the beginning of that year. I had just got out of a bad relationship, I lost myself. In fact, I no longer recognize myself anymore; I didn't even know who I was. My family turned completely against me as I grew closer to God. I had no one to turn to and I didn't want to live anymore. However, I have gone way past the depression stage. I didn't go anywhere anymore, I stop eating and I shut myself off from the outside world completely.

All I can remember is that one night I was driving, I kept having suicide thoughts. Although I didn't know what I was going to do but I was determined to commit suicide that night. So I kept crying and praying out to God. The next thing I know I heard the Holy Spirit for the first time in my life. I heard the voice of The Lord say "You can't do that because your son is in the car." At that moment, I turned the car around and I drove home. When I arrive home, I still had those same suicide thoughts in my mind so I took a bath. I cried out to God even harder so I got out the tub and fell on my knees on the side of my bed.

The next thing I know I felt someone hand touch my shoulder, that's when I realize everything was going to be okay. I felt so calm and peaceful for the first time in my life, that's when I realize it was Jesus Christ hand that touched my shoulder! It was a so bright around me and everything felt so new. God told me I had a purpose on my life and everything I went through was to make me stronger. So I said, "Yes God I surrender to your will, I will do whatever you want to do and I will say whatever you want me to say."

I meant every word I said that night and I never tried to commit suicide again. So woman of God, what I'm saying is no matter how hard life gets, you turned to God, remove the spirit of suicide away from your life. God has a purpose for your life, it doesn't matter what the world says or you say about yourself. You are who God says you are. In Genesis 1:27 "So God created man in his own image, in the image of God, created he him; male and female created he them."

No matter what situation you're in or what you go through in life, God is your only answer. There is no other option for you but God. Please do not commit suicide, you have to read your bible daily and speak the word of God over you lives daily. Listen to inspirational music, find a good church home that is led by the Holy Spirit, and surround yourselves around like minded Christians. Also, learn to trust God even more through hard times. God will always love you regardless of your past mistakes or failures, He is a forgiving God!

Have You Ever Felt Broken?

No one really knows the price of saying "Yes" to God! "Yes I surrender my life over to you and I will surrender to your will!" No one told you about the trial and tribulations you have to go through. Well, that's what happen to all God's chosen people and His anointed ones. You really have to go through Hell before you get to where God called you to be. Most prophets and apostles will tell you that.

That's not the problem, though; the problem is that most people give up before they leave out of the wilderness. God will take away everything you have just to humble you, get you that place and become the person He created you to be.

Oh but the scary part is that no one told you, you would lose everything you have but your dignity. No one told you, you will become homeless and sleeping on someone floor. No one told you, you will run out of money. No one told you, you will not even have enough money to put gas in your car or even take your child to McDonalds. In fact, no one told you about the lonely nights or the tears running down your eyes. Therefore, no one told you, you will not be able to buy your child clothes or shoes for school.

If it can't be worst, you found out a very close family member of yours has been murder. A week later a close friend of yours family member has been arrested for murder. Then you found out another family member is dying from an incurable disease and has less than a year to live.

Woman Of God: Who Did God Create You to Be?

But you never gave up, lost faith or lost hope, you found your strength from The Lord, you kept going from interviews to interviews but no one will hire you. Then you thought to yourself God said to trust and believe He would provide for you. But you wonder how, and then all of a sudden someone bought your child new clothes and shoes for school. They even bought your child school supplies for school.

You felt so thankful; you put your last ten dollars in church. The next day someone gave you a hundred dollars. You put fifteen dollars in church this time, and then someone gave you 320 dollars the next day. That same week someone else western union you 300 dollars, then someone else gave you 50 dollars to take your child to McDonalds and gas money for your car.

Oh but Christmas is right around the corner, you wonder how you're going to buy your child Christmas gifts. As a result on Christmas Eve as you were walking to your place, someone stopped you and noticed you had a child. He said "I know you have a child, I'm in the military and we give out Christmas toys. I had no one else to give them to and I was searching for someone all day but couldn't find anyone but then God led me to you." He walks you to his car, he has a truck full of toys and he gives them all to your child. It was more than your child ever had for Christmas and then your child birthday is right after Christmas. After that you start to receive checks in the mail from everywhere, you start to receive so much money from unexpected sources.

Oh but I'm not done yet, oh here come the haters because they see and know you are the one whom The Lord has blessed! They wonder how are you are able to do this or that but you don't have a job? What makes you so different from them? They curse you, call you terrible names and even talk about you behind your back. In fact, people think you are crazy and have lost your mind. Your own family turns against you, it seems like you have no one but God on your side. You wonder why they hate you but you realize you're not dealing with people you're dealing with spirits.

The closer you become to God, the devil will be on you even harder. He tries to stop the plans God has for you. In John 10:10 says "The thief comes only to steal and kill and destroy." In Luke 12:53 "The father shall be divided against the son and the son against the father; the mother against the daughter, and the daughter against the mother; the mother in law against her daughter in law, and the daughter in law against her mother in law."

You realize everything you have gone through was to humble you and make you stronger. You realize who your true provider is and where your natural source comes from. Now you know Jesus Christ is the way to overcome anything. In John 14:6 Jesus answered, "I am the way, the truth, and the life. No one goes to the Father except through me." The only way you can truly be saved is if you accept The Lord Jesus Christ as your Savior.

In 1 Corinthians 10:13 "The temptations in your life are no different from what others experience. And God is faithful. He will not allow the temptation to be more than you can stand. When you are tempted, he will show you a way out so that you can endure."

No matter what happens in your life, you can overcome anything. You are responsible for your own destiny in life. No one can stop you but yourself so now you are walking in your purpose in life and helping others to become closer to Jesus Christ.

Woman Of God: Who Did God Create You to Be?

    No matter what anyone else says, you know God is real. The only way you was able to come out of the darkness into the light, is because of our Lord Savior Jesus Christ. God made miracles happen into your life that others said was impossible. Now I ask you this question, have you ever really been broken?

Can I Trust You?

Can I trust you with my heart? Can I trust you with my life? Can I trust you not to leave me again? Will you stop separating yourself from me? Why do you keep distances yourself from me?

Therefore, I never wanted to give you my heart because I was afraid you will break my heart into pieces. I love you but I'm being patient with you.

In fact, I want to give you my love but you keep pushing me away from you. I want to be that submissive wife to you but you won't let me. You keep walking in and out of my life, but, this time, I want to give you my heart. Show me that you love me and you can be the husband to me that God created you to be.

Yes, my king I am scared and afraid but I'm willingly to let all my guards down to trust you.

But are you willingly to do the same thing? Can you trust me with your heart? Can you stop running away from me?

Are you willingly to let your guards down to give me your heart? Can you trust me with your heart? Can you commit to me as you have committed yourself to Christ? I'm ready to be that submissive wife to you as you submissive yourself to Jesus Christ!

In order for me to trust you, your actions have to show something different. In fact, I know you love me but what are you afraid of? Why do you keep running away from the person you love? Your heart cannot lie to you and I feel your connection so strongly.

Woman Of God: Who Did God Create You to Be?

You're no longer in the wilderness but you choose to live alone but God created a help mate for you. You either have a choice to choose love or be alone forever. You can't push everyone out your life but eventually, you will be alone. No one else is willingly to be patient with you or wait for you to finally be that husband that God created you to be.

My king pick wisely because your choices come with powerful consequences. Would you choose love that outweighed everything? Or would love be forced on you by God? God did not create a man to live alone.

God has already placed everything into place but I'm waiting on you so I can grow to trust you. It just doesn't happen overnight so show me signs to start trusting you. So right now "No" my king I do not trust you until you show me otherwise!

Woman Of God: Who Did God Create You to Be?

You Asked Me "Do I Love You?"

Well, the truth is that I have always loved you, I never stop loving you. When I first laid eyes on you, I thought you were quite handsome and you had a beautiful smile. When I walked through that door, I saw you watching me every time I came in there. I knew you liked me because I felt it. But I was concern about you because you always looked so sad and I wonder why?

When I was around you, I always enjoyed your presence and you made me so happy. Whenever you left me my presence, I felt so sad and lonely without you. I wanted you to hold me all day and night. You made me feel so safe but I didn't understand you.

Why was this handsome man so sad all the time? What is he hiding from me? Does he love me?

Every morning you would text me "I was beautiful" and then you would call me and the first thing you would say was "Hello Gorgeous, I love you." Every time I told you I love you, you always replied: "I love you more."

You saw me for what was on the inside of me, you love me for being me but not once did you ever try to have sex with me. You had respect for me and my body. You said you wanted more than that from me, you wanted my hand in marriage and you wanted to spend the rest of your life with me. So what was stopping you from fully committing yourself to me?

As a result, you were hurt from a previous relationship and your ex hurt you so bad and that damage you. I didn't understand that at the time so I left. It became so unbearable and I couldn't deal with all that heartache and pain from you so I gave up on us. We both had unresolved issues we never really dealt with.

    When I left you, I don't know what happen to you. You were no longer the same person and I didn't even know who you were anymore because I did not know this person. You have changed so much, you had so much resistance towards me and I felt like you no longer loved me. You start having sex with random strangers and that was not like you, you start smoking and drinking. You became so mean and hateful towards me.

    What I didn't expect to happen was for me to miss you the way I did. It hurts me so badly when I left you. I felt like I lost a part of me and I was missing my other half. Then I realize why I felt that way because my Adam had awakened and I am your missing rib, my love.

    We separate for about a year but you always reached out to me. I blocked you from every social media website but you always found a way to contact me. You chased me for a whole year. I asked you why you kept chasing after me and I kept ignoring you? Your answer was "You would never give up on love."

    So yes my love I still love you and I never stop loving you. No matter how hard I tried, it was always there. I tried dating other guys but it always failed because I was still in love with you. Sometimes I couldn't sleep at night I would feel you thinking about me so I would start praying for you.

    We have a special connection and both of our spirits have connected with each other. Although our natural bodies have never connected, I still feel the love you have for me. I see the sleepless nights you have because your mind is racing and you can't stop thinking about me. I see you praying at night asking God to bring me back to you and you would do anything in the world just to have me back in your life. I see you wishing you could be in my presence again so we can become one body in Christ. I see you battling within yourself and wondering are you ready to fully commit yourself to me? I know you have dreams about us getting married.

So yes my love I still love you, I never stop loving you. Yes, I forgive you, yes I would be your Esther and you would be my King. We can leave the past behind so we can move forward towards our future my love.

You Cannot Be GOD in A Person's Life

When I look into the mirror, I see a reflection of myself; I see the hurt and pain that she has to endure from you. What happen to her, how did she become so lost? Before she met you, she was filled with so much love and joy but you took that away from her.

Many may ask "why she keeps going back?" Is she a fool or is she just stupid? No, she is neither but she was a fool over love. How could she love someone so much that didn't love her back?

It was because of how he treated her, even though; he lied and cheated on her. She has never met a guy who was so nice to her and kindhearted to her. He was an older guy, he was so handsome, and he was good looking and tall. He had a nice body, a beautiful smile, pretty eyes, he had a good heart and he accepted her child as his very own child. Her child's father has just walked out their lives so he came at the right time.

He gave her expensive gifts, money, and everything, of course, her child as well. She fell head over heels for this guy and he was the most amazing guy she ever met. Although he lied to her, cheated on her, she still loved him. What she loves most about him was what was inside of him. Therefore, she knew he loved her and her child, but he was so lost on the inside. He was so hurt and damage from a previous relationship, he didn't know how to love her or even accept the love she had to offer him. Then she realizes he didn't love himself, so how could he love her? However, he had self-esteem issues as well.

Woman Of God: Who Did God Create You to Be?

In reality, he knew she was a good woman but he knew she deserves someone better than him. She was beyond beautiful, gorgeous on the outside and inside but he always felt like he wasn't good enough for her. He didn't want her to be with anyone else, but he was afraid of commitment towards her. He didn't want to lose her but he was too scared to settle down with her. Whenever she was not in his presence, he would lose his mind because he knew she was so beautiful and other guys would try to talk to her. Everywhere they went he would love to show her off but he still couldn't believe she was with him or that she really loved him. He would watch her, he saw all the attention she would get from other guys so that intimidate him even more.

Her family hates him, they always try to get her to date other guys, and they would never approve of him. They would say he don't do anything for you, he doesn't care about you or your child. He is a bad guy and you are a good girl. Why are you wasting your time with that loser? Her father told her not to marry him and he would never approve of him.

But they did not see what she saw on the inside of him, she could not help who she loved. She tried so hard to help him find his identity again but each time she tried, he would push her further away from him. However, she would pray for him when he was weak or when he couldn't pray for himself. In fact, she so focused on him, she forgot about herself. As a result, she no longer recognizes herself anymore; she didn't even know who she was. She became so depressed she tried to take her own life, but God saved her at the last minute. In the end, she left that toxic relationship because she realizes she could not be God in his life, he had to find God for himself.

God Loves You: But Are You Ready For Love?

When I needed you the most, you weren't there for me. When I told you I was hurting you didn't care, you only hurt me more. When I needed you to be strong for me, you were weak. You tried to hurt me anyway that you could.

But still I wasn't nothing but kind to you. You took my kindness for my weakness. Everything I gave you took it to hurt me until I had nothing left inside of me to give. All I know from you is lies and hurt because that's all you ever gave me. I hurt daily, my heart is broken but you never tried to repair it. You only damage me more; you only push me further away from you. You treated me like I was nothing to you and all you wanted to do was hurt me because you were hurting. You wanted me to hurt just as bad as you were hurting.

You think it's a game because you played with my heart. All I knew is lost and confusion because I lost myself. I no longer recognize myself anymore; you took everything of value I had to offer away. You no longer love me, you no longer cherish me, you no longer appreciate me, and you no longer knew my worth because I no longer knew my worth.

All I knew was the hurt and pain that you cause me to have. It became natural to me because that's all you ever showed me. So why you didn't love me it wasn't me that you didn't love, you didn't love your own self. You just wanted me to hurt because that's all you knew was hurt. You wouldn't allow me to love you because you didn't want to get hurt again.

Woman Of God: Who Did God Create You to Be?

But two people can't hurt each other they can only damage each other so a separation has to take place so both people can heal from broken hearts. It obviously that you two love each other so ask God for wisdom and guidance so you two can become one body in Christ!

Stop trying to hurt me and love me. Love me the same way that I love you. It's already inside of you because you can't sleep at night without thinking about me. In fact, you find yourself watching me on social media wondering how you could be so stupid to let me walk out your life. You're thinking I miss her so much, she is so beautiful but I wasn't ready for her and I didn't mean to hurt her. I really didn't want her to leave me. I know I will never find another woman like her so I have to do everything in my power to get her back. But this time, I won't lose her; I will be ready for her.

Therefore, I would do something I never did before. I will seek God for guidance and wisdom so I can be that Godly husband to her that she deserves. In fact, I will surrender my own life back over to Christ, ask Jesus to forgive me for my sins. However, I know I can't go back to her on my own; I will just hurt her all over again. So Jesus Christ be with me, wash me clean, make me pure and whole again. Open my eyes up so I can see and hear the way you do. Use me as your vessel so your will will be done in my life. Let me led her so she can submit to me as I submit to you Christ. Let me love her the way that you love her, don't never allow me to hurt her again.

Deliver me from all temptations, give me the strength to say no so I can love my wife the way she deserves to be loved. Lord please gives her a forgiving heart so she can forgive me. I love her; I don't want anyone else but her. So fix my eyes only for her, only allow me to love her and never hurt her again.

Now I forgive myself and now I finally love myself again. Thank you, Jesus, for giving me a second chance at life, let your will be done, not mine but let your will be done in my life in Jesus name! Amen! In Matthew 18:19 "Again I say unto you, That if two of you shall agree on earth as touching anything that they shall ask, it shall be done for them of my Father which is in heaven." And it is done in Jesus Name!

Is Money Really the Root Of All Evil?

In 1 Timothy 6:10 "For the love of money is the root of all kinds of evil. And some people, craving money, have wandered from the true faith and pierced themselves with many sorrows."

Money is not the root of all evil, being poor or living in poverty is the root of all evil. It simply states that the love of money is the root of all evil, not money but the love of money. People forget about God, lose faith and get too caught up in that lifestyle. People you rule the money, do not allow the money to rule you.

In 2 Corinthians 8:9 "For you know about the kindness or the grace of our Lord Jesus Christ. He was rich, yet for your sake, he became poor in order to make you rich through his poverty. Jesus Christ was poor so we may become rich." Jesus Christ was poor so we may become rich. Why people do not know this? Clearly they misunderstood this bible verse when people read their bible they would read it like it's a book instead of meditating on it. When you read your bible, you have to be led by the Holy Spirit in order to understand it. So I suggest you should stop reading the bible like it's a book because you should meditate on the word instead of just reading it.

Now if people had money, would the crime rate drop? People would rob, kill, steal and destroy for money but how can money be evil if people are dying trying to get it? As I stated earlier having money is not evil, not having money and living in a poor mindset is evil and full of ignorance.

Woman Of God: Who Did God Create You to Be?

In Matthew 6:9-10 9 "Our Father, which art in heaven, Hallowed be thy name. Thy kingdom come, Thy will be done in earth, as it is in heaven." This verse says that you can live in the kingdom of Heaven on Earth. Now it's one of the most popular scripture of the bible but people still skip the most important part. People do not understand it because they do not take time to study their bible.

People today would be the last day that you would live in a poor mindset. God already gave you the keys to access your wealth; you just have to get your life in order with God first.

How can God give you wealth when you do not believe you are wealthy? It's all starts with you and the way you think. If you have faith you are wealthy, then you will be wealthy. Go out in life, chase after your dreams, and find your purpose in life because your money is in your purpose in life.

Why would God give you money and you think it's evil? God would not give you money if you think its evil. God loves us; He knows we need money to survive that's why He created all the silver and gold to us. Jesus Christ does not want us to struggle or be broke. In fact, He knows we can't prosper without money so that's why He gives us access to Kingdom wealth on Earth.

Stop thinking money is evil, go out and reach your full prosperity in life to become the person God created you to be!

Overcoming Molestation

When people look at you, you wonder do they see the shame or the sadness that's hidden inside you. When people touch you or become too close to you, you feel fear or anxiety. You're afraid of people, you're fearful of everyone because you feel they would hurt you, just like a certain person hurt you when you were a child. Every time you walk out the door, you're very careful of your surroundings, you observe every detail about a person, and you watch them closely. Therefore, you keep yourself at a distance from everyone else. You try to hide yourself from the outside world; you make yourself seem unwanted because of the hurt that's inside of you. In fact, you feel like you're ugly, you're worthless, you're have no value in life and you feel like you do not belong here.

Therefore, you wonder why that happened to you when you were a child. Why did that man or woman hurt you? Why your parents wouldn't listen to you or why they didn't believe you? Now your life is a living hell, you're afraid of trusting people so you build a wall around you so you would not allow people to get in.

Therefore, I'm here to tell you, it was not your fault, you did not do anything wrong, you were a child. Do not give power to the person that hurt you so forgive yourself and the person that hurt you. You cannot live your life by being angry or mad all the time. I understand it might not be easy to forgive the person that sexually molested you when you were a child because it takes time to heal from something that hurtful. But I promise you it was not your fault, that man or woman was simply sick in the head and pray for that person to be healed by the blood of Jesus Christ.

Woman Of God: Who Did God Create You to Be?

As you slowly forgive that person, your life will start to become better. You will be able to live again and you will have peace in your heart that you never felt before. Now you will be filled with so much joy, love, tell your story to others so you can prevent it from happening to another child.

In life, we might not understand why certain things happen to certain people and not others but through it all, you cannot let it take control of your lives. As a result, you have to fight back and take back what's rightfully yours. Do not let another person take total control of your life but God.

You are who God created you to be. No longer will you have to walk around being ashamed or embarrassed. When you walk, you walk with your head held high now. You are no longer a victim, you are a survivor so open your mouth, speak with wisdom and force. Now you are walking, talking and being led by the Holy Spirit so no one can harm, hurt or damage you ever again.

From this day forward, you are a new person; you are now the person God created you to be. I decree and declare that everything that tried to destroy you or damage you is now defeated in the Name of Jesus. It can no longer conquer you unless you allow it to, so take your life back and live your life for Jesus Christ.

You are loved and you have the highest God on your side so nothing can stop. God created you to rule nations so go out tell your story to save other children from molestation or sexual abuse and help others to overcome it.

I Am the Woman Who God Called Me to Be

People you all do not know what I went through, I really went to Hell and back. But oh my God had a different story for me, God brought me out of the darkness into the light. People said I will fail, I will never amount to anything in life, I will be nothing because I have a child and I am not married. My whole family turned against me except for my Earthy Father and God. My family said I was crazy, stupid, they have lied on me, curses me out, and called me terrible names. They don't understand me, I'm no longer the same person and I am different from them. What they failed to realize was I was growing into the woman God called me to be. They wonder why I don't come around anymore, why I don't talk to them and why I don't do the things they do? But I refuse to settle for anything less and I don't need any negative energy in my life.

Yes I have a child and I am not married but God forgave me for that. I'm not perfect; God forgave me for my past. Jesus Christ said "I don't even remember your past anymore and if anyone bring up your past again, that is not me, it is from the enemy. The enemy will use your past against you to stop you from doing what I have called you to do." Therefore, my past is behind me, I refuse to go back to that lifestyle of sins and unhappiness. I was so lost, confused and I didn't even love myself anymore. I didn't want to live, I wanted to take my own life daily but God had other plans for me. God saved me when I didn't even want to save myself. There were days and nights I would cry, and ask God why I had to suffer?

Woman Of God: Who Did God Create You to Be?

God answered my prayers because my struggles only made me humble myself to be like Jesus Christ. God said "I love you, I have a purpose on your life, and I will use you to spread the gospel to many nations. My daughter you have a ministry on your life, you will rule many nations, you will bring people closer to me, help them to find their purpose in life and help them to become financially free." God, I'm not worthy enough, I have done some things in my past that I am not proud of and I am embarrassed about some of the things I did. Do not cry my child it's okay, now you can go out, tell your story to people so they will not make the same mistakes you have made. Now, my beautiful daughter I want you to tell your story to all nations through your writings. You are so beautiful; do not worry about your family or anyone else.

People do not define who you are; you are who I created you to be. I love you and your child; you will no longer struggle or be a single mother. I will send your husband to love you and your son. People can no longer hurt you or destroy you with their words; everyone who has caused you pain or hurt will perish. They will come back to you, they will need you, all of your enemies will bow you in the name of Jesus but you must forgive them so I can take you higher in life and promote you higher in life. No, my child you will not be alone because I will always be with you. You will forever be covered by the blood of Jesus Christ. God, I love you so much, I thank you for everything. I trust you all along, my family thought I was crazy but I knew I wasn't crazy.

I knew my family couldn't take me where you would lead me my Heavenly Father. I'm so graceful and thankful for everything you have done for me. I surrender to your will, I will do whatever you want me to do and I will say whatever you want me to say. I don't care what I have to go through, what I have to lose or give up. I give my life completely over to You God. My daughter everything is over with, you no longer have to struggle or suffer anymore, now I give you the Key to the Kingdom of Heaven on Earth. The gates of Heaven are open for you; you have kingdom connections to anywhere you want to go. No longer will you have to fear or be afraid, people will know I am with you, you will bless others as they will bless you.

 My daughter, you have been so faithful to me when others told you give up, but you did not give up. I love you for being a faithful servant, so everything you have lost I will replace it with a 100 fold more. I will prosper, multiply and double everything you do. You are in your prosperity season and your suffering season is over with. Everything in your old life is dead, it's gone, I have removed everything and everyone that did not belong in life your anymore. Your new life is filled with so much love, joy, abundance, and peace. Your child has kept you safe, he protected you when no one else would so I will bless him for doing that and I will bless your Father for not giving up on you when everyone else did. Your family will be blessed through you and all the ones that hurt you will no longer hurt you anymore. They will all reach out to you but you must have a forgiving heart so I can send you into the promise land that I have called you to. I love you my beautiful daughter, always remember my words, stand strong my child and know I will always be walking with you because you are a walking bible!

A Single Mother Cry

When you look at her, all you see is a beautiful face but that beautiful face shields so many tears and lonely nights. No one told her all the sacrifices she will have to make for her son or how hard it was to be a single parent. She never imagines in her lifetime that she will be a single mother. But that's only the beginning because God will send her a God fearing husband to accept her son as his own child. When she walks, no one told her that she would struggle to get to the top. But her life shouldn't be like this because she grew up with a silver spoon in her mouth so what went wrong in her life. Well, nothing went wrong in her life, the closer you get to God, and the devil will be on you even more. In John 10:10 "The thief comes only to steal and kill and destroy. I came that they may have life and have it abundantly."

The enemy knows the plans God has for you so he tries to stop it before you are even able to reach your destiny in life. It's sad because many people fall for his trap but not Christy Sanderson because all her struggles in life made her stronger and wiser so don't let her cute face fool you. She will not let the enemy win or take control of her life; she has come too far to give up on God now. What God has done for her in her life, couldn't nobody have done it but God. Where she is at in her life right now took time. It just didn't happen overnight. She made time for God on sleepless nights when she couldn't sleep at night. She would write letters to God and He would speak to her. There were days when she didn't even know which way to go but she knew Jesus Christ so she went to him. As a result, she did not go to anyone else because no one else could help her or work it out but God. It was days when she felt like she had nothing to give so she gave God her heart, she did not have money but she gave what she did have. She had no excuses so she went to her Heavenly Father.

People look at her, all they saw was a lifestyle but they don't see her struggles, heartache or pain. However, she gave her life completely over to The Lord. Therefore, she didn't care if she failed or not, she lost so much but each time God always double what she lost. Failure was not an option for her because God always promoted her higher. She learned what it was like to live by faith and not an income. God told her to leave her homeland because she will rule many nations. All along she was building a nation without a bank account. God was her source of income, she depend on God like never before. He increases her income dramatically but she always sowed seeds and helps others on the way. So don't tell me what my God can't do. The same thing God did for Abraham, Isaac and Jacob, He will do it for you. You just have to have the faith of Abraham.

A Single Mother

When I was growing up, I always wanted to be a wife. I dream about the wedding day, my career and having our first kids. I never imagine or dream I would be a single mother. I never thought I would have my first child at the young age of nineteen. But who knew all my sins would catch up with me or all my actions came with powerful consequences. Oh, I never imagine I will be raising a son without a father.

When I first found out I was pregnant, I was more shocked than anything. I was scared but I knew I had to have my baby and take full responsibility of my baby. How did I get pregnant? I know we always asked that question but, to be honest, I don't even remember the night or day I became pregnant. I thought to myself I wasn't ready to be a mother and from the first day, I found out I was pregnant I knew I was going to be a single mother. To be honest, my biggest fear in life was I will forever be a single mother but God told me something. "If I fully commit my spirit into The Lord, obey all of His commandments, He will send me a Godly fearing husband to love me and my son as his very own child!" "For no eye has seen, no ear has heard, no mind has conceived the wonderful things that God has prepared for those that love Him" (1 Corinthians 2:9).

When I found out I was having a boy, I was very surprised because my parents had all girls and it's mostly women in my family. I was thinking to myself, what am I going to do? I can't raise a boy into a man. In fact, my family made sure they kept telling me a woman cannot raise a boy into a man. As a result, I told myself I might not be able to raise my son into a man but with God on my side I will do my very best and be the best mother to my son until God sends my husband into our lives. In Proverb 22:6

Woman Of God: Who Did God Create You to Be?

"Train up a child in the way he should go; even when he is old, he will not depart from." No, it's not easy being a single mother but that is my fault because I chose to have sex outside of marriage but I knew what to do to prevent it from happening again because I'm saving my body for my husband only. Yes, I had to make sacrifices for my son but that is okay because my son is a blessing and I'm thankful to have my child in my life. He gives me so much joy and makes me so happy. When I'm sad, he brightens my day and he always says something to put a smile on my face. "The Lord is my helper, I will not be afraid. What can man do to me?" (Psalm 118:6) or "I can do all things through Christ who strengthens me." (Philippians 4:13) He will help provide tangible reminders of His love and protection when things get tough or stressful. So what I'm saying if you are a single mother, do not lose faith because it's still hope for you. It might not seem like it but trust me God haven't forgotten about you. All God wants is your love, praise and for you to worship Him.

    I don't care what it looks like; God can change everything around in three days. If you are a struggling mother, just know struggle means greatness is inside of you and God is preparing you for your husband. Do not be focus on your situation or your future husband, keep your eyes on Jesus Christ and watch how your life will change around for the better. I decree and declare that you shall be the Godly woman God called you to be, you will be the mother of many nations and you are the Proverb 31 woman. Do not lose sight woman of God, do not let loneliest interfere with your destiny in life. In your time of singleness keep your eyes focus on Jesus Christ. A man should pursue you and you should never pursue a man. In Proverb 18:22 "He who finds a wife finds a good thing and obtains favor from the LORD."

Who Shall Separate You from The Love of God?

When I look into the mirror I see a reflection of me, I recognize that it was me in my new transformation. Who is this woman? She is not the same person she was last year. No one shall separate her from the love of God. No one can come to her unless they come through God first. Why does she have such a shield of protection from God around her? She surrenders her life over to God and let Him take total control of her life. The Holy Spirit guides and leads her when she has no idea where she is head to next. Many wonder about her, they can't understand her and they are always trying to figure her out! She stands out from everyone else but some women envy her while others love her. All the guys love and adore her. Her family disowns her because she is different and they don't even know who she is anymore. She is so unrecognizable because she is so delighted into The Lord. Her natural born father has always been there for her and he is the only true person in her family besides her son that truly loves her. As a result, her family wonders why she can't go back to her old sinful ways, and be like them.

Therefore, she refuses to go back to her old sinful ways because they can't give her the joy she has now. Only Jesus Christ can give her unconditional love and God has brought her out of the wilderness into the light. Now they hate her because she out shines and out stands them. But the only difference between them and her is that she let the Holy Spirit led the way for her. She accepts the calling of Jesus Christ calling her higher. In fact, they only see her struggles but oh no they ignored the blessings. God has blessed her with true abundance and life. She lives in the supernatural and not in the natural world. Oh but now her family thinks she is crazy, stupid might even lost her mind but they don't understand that Jesus Christ is right there with her and she only has the mind of our Lord Savior. Therefore, she had to learn whom to listen to and not to listen to. God sent more Godly people into her life and then all of a sudden God starts to use her to change nations and to make a legacy. However, she finally became delivered from people and, of course, her family. It didn't take her long to realize her family couldn't take her where God was leading her, only our Lord Savior himself could do that.

Of course her family talks about her behind her back, call her hurtful names, curse her out or even makeup lies about her because they can't find anything negative to say about her but who cares because no one can separate her from the love of God. No matter what she does a person, her family or anyone else will try to destroy her but it doesn't matter because it won't work. In Psalms 105:15 God says "Do not touch my anointed ones; do my prophets no harm." As long as she keeps the love of God in her heart, everyone that tries to destroy her shall perish. Now people including her family members or anyone else that ever doubt her will truly know she is the one whom The Lord has blessed! No one shall separate her from the love of God!

Trust Issues

Trusting people is the hardest thing for you to do. You have trust issues and you don't even realize it. Every time someone tries to get close to you, you reject them before they can get a chance to even know you. When they give you compliments, you don't know how to receive it because you feel like you are not good enough or not worthy enough to accept it.

You try to hide your true self from a certain person but this person sees right through you. As a result, you try to act like everything is fine and you having everything together but deep down you are hurting on the inside.

You're not happy, you have so much hurt on the inside of you but yet you have to keep your guard up. So many people have let you down and betrayed you in the past. When you really needed them the most, they turned their backs on you and shut you off completely. People have used you, took your kindest for your weakest, mistreated you and used you for money. They took everything that you had until you had nothing left to give.

People have a laugh at you, talk about you in front of your face but mostly behind your back. They can't find anything negative to say about you so they make up lies about you. It hurts you and you wonder why they talk about you. They talk about you because you are different and you do not think the same way they think. You trust God, walked out on faith and follow all your dreams in life. Do not worry why you don't fit in with everybody because you are not meant to fit in with everybody. God made you stand out from everyone else and that's why you are different from everyone else.

Woman Of God: Who Did God Create You to Be?

No wonder you don't trust anyone but you have to let go of your past in order to move with forward with your future. You can't hide from people or just shut everyone off. That person you are trying to avoid or stay away from is probably the person you need the most. God will send people in your life to help you, strengthen you and to bring you closer to Jesus Christ. Not all people are out to hurt you or drain you emotionally. Some people are really generally good people and will never do anything to hurt you.

Although you do not connect with your blood family or so called friends but you will always connect with your spiritual family. When you meet this person you never met him/her a day in your life but you connect with this person instance and you feel like you have known this person all of your life. That's because you are both connected in the spirit and now you have access to your spiritual family.

So basically, what I'm saying is its okay to let your guard down sometimes and let people in. Some people really have good intentions for you and think you are the most amazing person they ever met. Stop shutting people off and let them get to know the real you because the only person you're hurting is yourself. But most importantly give your trust and heart to people that deserves it. Seek God to replace that empty void inside of you and learn to love yourself and know your true self-worth. God created you in his very own image and He loves you so much! You are the way God created you to be so it's okay to let people in. Don't try to build relationships with people so fast, just stop, take your time and slowly let things happen the way they are supposed to happen.

I Saw My Angel

When I looked in the mirror, tonight I saw my angel. She is so beautiful, gorgeous and she was so happy. She smiled at me and she was full of joy. When I looked in the mirror I saw her inside of me, I never saw anything like her before. Her eyes are so big and pretty. She is beyond beautiful on the inside and outside. My angel out shines everyone; she has such a powerful glow on her and a powerful presence inside of her. In fact, she is flawless; however, her beauty is beyond this world can explain. This world cannot explain to her because she is a woman that is after God's very own heart.

Her name is Christy which means beautiful, graceful princess and a follower of Christ! How did she see her angel but yet she is living in this harsh, cruel world. It wasn't her angel that she saw face to face it was her spirit because she is living in the supernatural and being led by the Holy Spirit.

Therefore, she shall live and not die; God revealed to her that things she thought was dead inside of her shall live. God has risen her back up again and she shall live and not die. She lives by faith and not by sight because she is a walking bible living on earth. No one can stop her because God is protecting her and she shall defeat all of her enemies. She will have the last laugh and everyone that doubt her shall perish. God will always have the last word.

This woman is on a mission, she will lead nations to accept Jesus Christ as their Lord and Savior. As a result, she will also lead others to financial freedom and to reach their wealth zones. She will not be put to shame or hide out any longer. God has shown her true identity and He will no longer hide her. Our Lord God has brought her out of the shadow of death to raise her up higher. God is calling her higher. God said hear my voice, see my face and harden not your heart. My child I am calling you higher.

    This woman shall not settle for anything less than her worth because she is so precious in my eyes. My beautiful daughter is created in my very own image and I love her so much. I am proud of the young woman she has matured to be. Her worth is far more valuable than any rubies, diamonds or any expensive jewels. She shall not lack or go without anything in her life. Riches and wealth follow her everywhere she goes and she has entered her wealth zones.

    However, this woman must keep her eyes focus on Jesus Christ no matter what. She has to remain a woman that is after God's heart or she will become unbalance. She must not follow the wicked ways of this world. She will continue to be led by the Holy Spirit all the days of her life.

    So my question for you is you willing to give up everything and be a woman after God's very own heart? Do not be afraid because God is always with you and He will never leave you nor forsake you. How would you like to see your angel and meet her face to face? Your angel is already inside of you, you just have to seek God in order to find her!

Sex Outside of Marriage

People do understand or are not aware of the true dangers of sex outside of marriage. In 1 Corinthians 6:18 "Flee from sexual immorality. All other sins a man commits are outside his body, but he who sins sexually sins against his own body." 1 Corinthians 10:8 "We should not commit sexual immorality, as some of them did – and in one day twenty-three thousands of them died."

It was never God's plan for our lives to have sex outside of marriage. It is meant for two people that are husband and wife. When husbands and wives joints together they become one body in Christ.

However, when two people are not married it increases the risks of STDs and HIV/AIDS and people are dying daily of an incurable disease. It says that in the bible that people will die from having sex outside of marriage. It is very important to wait until you are married to have sex, it's okay if you have been sexually active in your life because you can take your pureness back. You can practice being celibate and trust me you will feel so much better.

Although it cause death to some people outside of marriage but that is not the main reason you should wait for marriage to have sex. People, did you know every person you have sex with outside of marriage brings ungodly soul ties?

1 Corinthians 5:9 "I have written you in my letter not to associate with sexually immoral people." 1 Corinthians 6:16, "What? Know ye not that he which is joined to a harlot is one body? For two, saith he, shall be one flesh."

Woman Of God: Who Did God Create You to Be?

In this verse, the two people did not get married but their bodies connected spiritual when their bodies joined together from sex outside of marriage. Therefore, that was created for them to have ungodly soul ties. Okay think about it there was a time in your life where you had a one night stand with a person and years later that person still comes to your mind. That is because of the soul tied that was created.

In fact, it not only brings ungodly soul ties but it brings demonic spirits as well. When a person has demons spirits in them, it can transfer their body into yours as well because you are both connected in the spirit. It also brings emotional stress and it ruins relationships with people.

Take a quick second think about a time when you was close friends with someone of the opposite sex, one night you both end of having sex and it ruined you both friendship. That person no longer acts the same around you, now that person distances themselves away from you, is now ignoring and avoiding you at the same time. Therefore, you now feel hurt and rejected by that person. This person has damaged your body and self-esteem. Now you feel lonely and depressed because you gave your body to that person and you can't take it back.

As a result, you are hurting and looking for love in all the wrong places. So you meet someone else, you give your body up to that person but that void that is inside of your heart is still there. You never healed from the first person that hurt you so it becomes a pattern for you all over again. You searched for love and keep searching but every person you meet end up hurting you all over again. You can never be happy until you conquer that same mountain.

Stop having sex outside of marriage, stop giving your bodies to strangers. God is the only person that can heal you from all the hurt and pain. Jesus Christ is the only person that can fill that empty void that is inside of your heart. It all starts with you first, give your life back to God and take control of your life again.

That is not a part of God; if someone wants to have sex with you outside of marriage, you don't need them anyway. A true person of God will not approach you in that way, that person knows and understands the importance of marriage before sex. Therefore, when you choose to save sex for marriage, you avoid all the negatives things in life. If you're dealing with consequences from sex outside of marriage or already have gone too far physically, there is still hope. You can start fresh to avoid these dangers from this point on through the gift of starting over and giving God your life all over again, you can still have a second chance in life.

My Husband Went Through God First

When I look into your eyes, I see a man of courage and complete integrity. When I open my eyes, I see the most handsome man and the most beautiful smile. You are a man of God but you haven't found your identity yet. You're holding on to your past but you must let it go to move forward with your life.

Oh, I wish you could see the man I see inside of you. I don't care about your past I just love you for you. It's something so special about you but I don't know what it is. I just know I love you and you're the most amazing guy I ever met.

Whenever I'm around you, words cannot even come out my mouth because I never met a man like you before. My love, you always wonders why I'm so quiet around you but I don't know what to say to you because I know you were sent from God to me.

Oh, my love you knew I was your wife the moment you first laid eyes on me when I first walked through that door. You knew I was the wife you have been praying for the night before you met me. When I enter the room, my presence was so powerful and you could see the Glory of God shining all over me.

Your heart was beating so fast but yet it was filled with so much joy. You were thinking God I prayed for a wife but this woman was more than what I prayed for. She is a blessing but I didn't expect to meet her so soon and for her to be so gorgeous. Her heart is pure, her hair is so long, and she is so well groomed and fashionable dress.

Woman Of God: Who Did God Create You to Be?

My love, you prayed for a wife so God answered your prayer. When I look at you, I see a man whom has been hurt from his past but he tries to hide who he truly is from me. So I ask God, how can I find this man and get to him? God says "The only way he can come to you is that he has to come through me first before he comes to you, my child."

Wow God this man is my husband I just know it because I see the visions of us being married and I can feel it in my heart. Oh, my child just knows he loves you, he is your husband but in this season I am teaching you to be patient.

Father God I know I have to be patient but I can't help the way I feel about this man. He is the most incredible guy I ever met. I love the way he challenges me to make me stronger and how he leads me closer to my dreams in life. When I am weak, he is strong for me. Whenever I am in his presence, I feel the love he has for me. When he hugs me or when we touch hands it feels like we are already one body in Christ. He has the most beautiful smile I have ever seen but God I know he is hurting right now but he can get through this. I will continue to guide him towards you so he can be led by the Holy Spirit. Jesus Christ, I know he has to come to you first before he comes to me. God give him the strength where he is weak and deliver him from temptation.

My Lord, please do not allow him to forget me or my presence in his life in Jesus Name. Lord please gives him dreams and visions so he will remember me. Do not allow him to forget that I am the wife you send to him and I am his wife that he prayed for the night before. Keep his eyes fix on me and no one else. Lord continues to guide and led him to the right direction so he can come to you.

Woman Of God: Who Did God Create You to Be?

Do not allow him to settle for anything less so he can be that Godly husband to me that you created him to be.

Father God I know this man was sent from you because I would not have picked him for myself. I never knew a man like him could exist in real life. Jesus Christ, I love you so much but I know I cannot love this man more than I love you. I know I have to love God more than I love this man. I will forever love this man and I will never stop loving him. When he do not want me to love him, I stand strong for him and I am praying for him when he can't even pray for himself.

Lord bring this man to you so you can heal his wounded heart; take away all his headaches and pains. Cover my husband by the blood of Jesus Christ, protect him and keep guard from the world. Find him and do not allow my love to get lost or confused in this world. Console him, bring him to You Lord and I will wait patiently as his wife in this season just like you told me to Father God.

So my question to you is, do you know this man? This man is Jesus Christ and no man shall come to you unless he comes through Jesus Christ first and then he can come to you to be your husband in one body in Christ!

Spend Time with God

What do I mean about spending time with God and how can you spend time with God? You cannot function correctly without spending time with God. Give God your time; it must be done because without God you are nothing.

How can you start your day off property and you can't even speak to The Lord when you first wake up the morning. Your day is out of order from the start so therefore, your life has been out of order for a while because you cannot speak to the one who created you. What is wrong with you, get your life back in order and give Jesus Christ your time. If it's simply thank you father for waking me up this morning, say something to God so your day is in order and you will have a peaceful morning.

When you do not pray or spend time with God, you let evil spirits enter into your body and they come to destroy and kill you. Evil spirits or demons run by the name of Jesus so make Jesus Christ a priority in your life. God must be first in your life no matter what; He comes first before your child or even your family. Everything has to line up with the word of God before you even start your own family.

Without our Lord Jesus in your life you will be lost, searching for answers but can never find peace or happiness. The world can't give you joy or peace only God can do that.

No matter how busy you are, make time for God and find a quite peaceful place just to pray and talk to God. Do not do the entire talking, listen to God and write down whatever He speaks to your heart. God will respond back because the more time you spend with God, you will hear

Him more clearly. In fact, take your bible with you and He will even guide you to certain verses in the bible to read.

When I first start getting close to God I would write Him a letter every day, I will tell him about my day and how I was feeling. It made me feel so much better. Then after a while, I notice when I start writing more letters, it was no longer about my day. God was telling me about myself and revealing the real Christy Sanderson to me. I could hear, feel, and see things more clearly. As a result, I because sensitive to the spirit and I was thinking more like God. The Lord will tell me things that I had to change about my life and how to improve in certain areas about my life. Then He starts revealing things to me about my family that I never knew and then about other people lives.

Jesus was really working miracles in my life. I was praying so much, my son was four at the time he starts praying with me and he learn to hear the voice of God. My son will tell me things and it will come true.

That's why I said you must spend time with God so you can be led by the Holy Spirit and know the voice of God. When you are being led by the Holy Spirit, you will be so happy just to spend time with God it will become a part of your daily lives.

One time I spend a whole day with God, I was so excited and happy just to give God my time and to spend the day with my Father. Jesus has done some amazing and powerful things in my life but He isn't finish with me yet. No matter how I was feeling or what mood I was in, I will give God all my time.

The more time you spend with God, He will bless you with so much more than you ever imagine. The Lord loves you so much, He wants your time and He wants you to come to Him for everything. In John 14 13-14 "And whatsoever ye shall ask in my name, that will I do, that the Father may be glorified in the Son. If ye shall ask any thing in my name, I will do it."

Know Your Worth

  Woman of God, Jesus Christ paid the price for your body so treat your body like it is a temple. In 1 Corinthians 6:19-20 "Or do you not know that your body is a temple of the Holy Spirit within you, whom you have from God? You are not your own, for you were bought with a price. So glorify God in your body." In 1 Corinthians 3:16-17 "Do you not know that you are God's temple and that God's Spirit dwells in you? If anyone destroys God's temple, God will destroy him. For God's temple is holy, and you are that temple." Why are you dressing half naked and sleeping with strangers?

  Woman of God stop lowering your standards by having sex with every man that wants you. A man won't respect you if he has sex with you the first night he meets you. He will see you as being easy and a play toy. The only time he calls you is late at night when his main woman is not around. Don't settle being the other woman, when God made you a wife for someone else.

  You should walk and talk with the spirit and cover of God; therefore, everywhere you go you should leave your mark of blessings. Stop gossiping and speaking negative things, your mouth should be shut off of all evil things. Jesus Christ paid the price for our sins so depend on him like you never did before, save your lives so you won't have to suffer Hell on Earth.

  Woman of God be the woman God called you to be so you can get your Godly Husband! If you stop searching for love in all the wrong places and start searching for God than things will change for the better in your lives. If a man doesn't love God, you don't need him. The only way a man will truly love you is one that is after God's heart. A man should love God more than he loves you. He made that covet with God just like Jesus Christ did with his body in the church. A man should lead you and not break you. He should love, care, appreciate you and put you first in his life but as I stated earlier this man of God loves God more than he loves you.

In Ephesians 5: 25 "Husbands, love your wives, just as Christ loved the church and gave himself up for her." In Ephesians 5: 28 "In this same way, husbands ought to love their wives as their own bodies. He who loves his wife loves himself." In Ephesians 5:31-33 "The Scripture says, so a man will leave his father and mother and be united with his wife, and the two will become one body. That secret is very important- I am talking about Christ and the church. But each of you must love his wife as he loves himself, and a wife must respect her husband."

Woman of God you're praying for a Godly husband but you don't even know your worth is far more precious than rubies or diamonds. Now, why would God send you a Godly husband when your life is corrupt? You show your body everywhere on the internet, you're always half naked dress, you use fool language, you're at the club every weekend, you drink, smoke, and your mother is raising your children. What kind of woman are you, you're not that woman anymore so act likes the woman God made you to be and be that Proverb 31 type of woman.

A woman is not supposed to act like she is desperate for a man or an attention seeker. Act like you have some class and know your value is far greater than that. Stop settling for these so called no good men that continue to lie to you, cheat on you and hurt you all over again. A man should pursue you and you should never pursue a man. If a man wants you, he will find a way to make you his only one. He will do everything in his power to keep you and will never do anything to hurt you or make you leave him. This man knows what he has, he has been praying to God for someone like you and he knows God send you to him.

Woman of God learn to be submissive wives during your time of singleness, keep your focus on God. Do not try to play the man in the relationship and do not try to dominate the man. A man is supposed to lead his household and not the woman. In Ephesians 5:22-24"Wives, submit yourselves to your own husbands as you do to the Lord. 23 For the husband are the head of the wife as Christ is the head of the church, his body, of which he is the Savior. 24 Now as the church submits to Christ, so also wives should submit to their husbands in everything.

The Spirit of Poverty

God did not create us to live in poverty. In 2 Corinthians 8:9 9 "For ye know the grace of our Lord Jesus Christ, that, though he was rich, yet for your sakes he became poor, that ye through his poverty might be rich." Jesus Christ became poor so we can become rich. God did not make us to be poor so that's why He gives us ideas to start our own business but our business must line up in the Kingdom of God. Our business are meant to help people and bring many people closer to Jesus Christ as we can but not to harm people or use them to get their money.

In Deuteronomy 28:12-13 "The LORD shall open unto thee his good treasure, the heaven to give the rain unto thy land in his season, and to bless all the work of thine hand: and thou shalt lend unto many nations, and thou shalt not borrow.13 And the LORD shall make thee the head, and not the tail, and thou shalt be above only, and thou shalt not be beneath; if that thou hearken unto the commandments of the LORD thy God, which I command thee this day, to observe and to do them." God said you will lend too many nations and never borrow from them. He has made you the Head and not the tail. In Matthew 6:10 "Thy kingdom come. Thy will be done in earth, as it is in heaven."

Jesus Christ said our will be done on earth as it is in Heaven. So we can live in the Kingdom of Heaven on Earth. Now if Jesus Christ said all of this, why do we have so many people living from pay check to pay check and struggling to pay their bills?

People are scared to walk out on faith, have a lack of faith and do not trust God. As a result, people rely on man instead of God. Think about it 90 percent of the world wants an hourly salary job because it is supposed to be more stable and it has a fixed income so therefore it is easier and safer to live that way. However, whoever told you that is a Lie because when you live like that you put a limit on how much money you can make and you also put a limit on what God can do. God will never put a limit on our income because He knows we need money to spread his word to all nations. Jesus Christ will supply our every need but He cannot do that if we put a limit on what He can do for us. The Lord said we are all a part of Abraham's seed and we are blessed through the promise He made to Abraham. Therefore, Abraham seeds are blessed and rule many nations.

Why would you settle and God has something so much better for you. You settle because you trust man instead of God, so you work at the same place for over a decade and never get a promotion or some cases you might not even get a raise. People settle because they are too lazy and make excuses for themselves. If God already put the millionaire/billionaire potential inside of you, go out and do it. The same way you hustle in the streets, go out and make some legal money so you can keep young men out of prisons cells. Who cares what people says? Okay so what you fail the first time, go out and try again. If it didn't work one way, find another solution until it does work. Do not quit, try harder, and be commited to it. I promise you if you just try and do your part, God will open doors for you.

In Revelation 3:7-8 "When God opens a door, no one can close it. And when he closes it, no one can open it. I know what you do. I have put an open door before you, which no one can close. I know you have a little strength, but you have obeyed my teaching and were not afraid to speak my name."

Woman Of God: Who Did God Create You to Be?

Oh wait but you're still making excuses; you don't have any money to start your own business! That's why you start off with what you have; you have to start from the bottom to get to the top. Most millionaires/billionaires were poor and homeless but look at them now. They did not give up, they made a way out of no way, they started off with nothing and you would have never known they were homeless.

Sometimes God will allow the spirit of poverty to attack us to make us stronger and more humble. Now that you have experienced the spirit of poverty, you know what to do to prevent it from happening again. If God trusts you with little money, now He is going to change the way you think, and change your lifestyle around so you can be wealthy!

The Spirit of Homosexuality

A lot of people are afraid to discuss this topic and really do not know where to begin with this topic that it must be spoken. It's sad to say but society is so judgmental and really treats these people like outsiders, especially the so-called Christians and people in the church.

Let me tell you about the spirit of homosexuality. When a man is attractive to the same sex, it is a spirit of a gay man inside of him or when a woman is attractive to someone of the same sex, it is a spirit of gay women inside of her. A lot of people are not even award of the fact it is an evil spirit attached to that man/woman. Did you know that the homosexuality is one of the hardest spirits to fight off because that spirit constantly attaches itself to that person? This person is constantly battling with itself of this man/woman and they might really want to change deep down inside but they don't know how or where to begin. Each time that person try to take a step to change, that homosexuality spirit leaves that person body and comes right back with seven more evil spirits.

In Matthew 12:43-45 "When the unclean spirit is gone out of a man, he walketh through dry places, seeking rest, and findeth none. 44 Then he saith, I will return into my house from whence I came out; and when he is come, he findeth it empty, swept, and garnished. 45 Then goeth he, and taketh with himself seven other spirits more wicked than himself, and they enter in and dwell there: and the last state of that man is worse than the first. Even so shall it be also unto this wicked generation." This evil spirit does this because the devil knows that God did not create people to have sex with the same sex. The enemy knows that this sin is one of the worst sins you can commit and knows it will send you to Hell.

Woman Of God: Who Did God Create You to Be?

In Leviticus 20:13 "If a man also lie with mankind, as he lieth with a woman, both of them have committed an abomination: they shall surely be put to death; their blood shall be upon them." Satan used this spirit to send people to Hell because he knows he cannot defend God and the only way he can hurt God is through his people. God never intend for his people to go to Hell so the devil used the spirit of homosexuality to send as many as God's people to Hell as he can, then laugh in their faces and tell them they could have lived for God but they ignored God's teachings and commandments. Did you know it is a place in Hell where the fire burns and tortures are seven times worst for people who are attractive to the same sex? If you're not sure or believe what I am talking about I urge you to read Mary K. Baxter book "A Divine Revelation of Hell"

How can you help this person when you keep rejecting, judging them or won't allow them in the church? Remember we all sin but others help us to change along the way so why you won't allow this person in your church because he/she is gay. That is wrong and hateful in the eyes of God. There was a point of time when you were battling or struggling with something that is a sin but no one rejects you. God forgave you for your sins so why you can't forgive this person and show them the steps you took to change your life around.

Instead of rejecting this person, take the proper steps to help that person change and guide them along the way. You never know what a person went through or know their story or understand why they are gay all of a sudden now. Many people do things and they don't even understand why they are doing it. Majority of the time something happens to them while they were a child, they never told anyone or never knew how to deal with the situation. So they go through life thinking it is their fault, they blame themselves, their parents and be wondering where God was while this was happening to them.

A lot of people do not deal with these issues because they don't know how to change or where to begin. That's why it is so important to talk to people, get to know them, meet them at their level and be led by the Holy Spirit. Majority of these churches are so stuck in traditions and religious they forget the church is the body of Jesus Christ and it is supposed to change people lives and bring them closer to God.

In some cases it might be different, remember what I said earlier about people rejecting them in the church; however, some people just want to be accepted and loved by society. All their lives people always judge them, mistreat them about their appearance so they join the homosexuality community because they are the ones that accept them and did not reject them. People will do things they are not proud of or do not like just to say they have someone to say they love them and accept them as they are.

Men and women of God forgive yourselves first, it is not your fault, you were just a child and you cannot change what happen to you. Acknowledge the fact that it did happen to you, talk to God about it, tell Him about how you felt about that person validating you and taking your childhood away. Forgive that person that hurt you and God will fill that empty void that has been missing inside of you since you were a child. Men/women of God regardless of what society says God still loves you and He has already forgiven you for your sins of your past. God will meet you right where you are and you can change. Don't worry about what society think about you, say about you or try to bring up your past because God has already forgotten about them. If you are willing to change, I mean if you really want to change all you have to do is take the steps and try. If you do your part too, God will do the rest for you.

    Yes God still loves you and He will send you a Godly spouse of the opposite sex to love you regardless of your past. God has something so much better that He has to offer you. It might not be an easy road to take, it is a process you have to take, but you must remain strong through it all and you can conquer that homosexuality spirit. You can do that by praying, fasting and surround yourselves around Godly people who is higher at your level with God. You must also be at a church that is led by the Holy Spirit instead of a man because you must be around people who is there to help you instead of judging you.

Stop Trying to Figure out whether That Person is real or fake

You're so busy trying to figure out if this person is real or not and that's all you focus on. Your main focus should be on Jesus Christ. Every time you hear or see prophets, apostles, evangelists and pastors on television, you always say that man or woman isn't real. How do you know if they are real or fake? You're too busy trying to prove that this person is fake instead of focusing on God. You spend more time trying to prove this person wrong instead of focusing on getting yourself better and becoming the image of Jesus Christ.

Who cares if that person is real or not? God will punish that same man/woman that pretends to be someone else. Our Lord Jesus Christ already know who is real or not, so stop discussing whether this person or that person is real.

People get so caught up in the media that they envy God's people and find every little detail about that person and make it seem like this person is so wrong. In reality, they are jealous of that same person that they try to prove wrong because that person is fulfilling their purpose for God while they are sitting at home not doing anything productive with their lives. When God created us, he created all of us with a purpose; it's just up to us to find out what that purpose is.

If you spend less time trying to prove that this person or that person isn't real and spend more time with God, you will start receiving blessings just like that other person. The more time you spend with God, the more Jesus

Christ will shine through you. People will see you as being blessed and they will know that you are the one whom The Lord has blessed.

Keep your eyes, ears fix on Christ, you will see with your spiritual eyes; hear and God will reveal people's true identity to you. What you see will shock you because the main ones you said are fake are truly God's people and the ones you thought was God's people are really a part of the devil. Watch what you say because the closer you get to God, you will see people true identities and it will not be a pretty sight. So I advise you to keep your focus on Jesus Christ and nothing else because if you don't, you will get hurt in the end. One thing you don't do is to touch God's anointed ones and do no harm to his prophets because you will get burn in the end!

Break Every Chain

I see an army rising up; there is an army of young people rising up to break all generation's curses. There is an army rising up to break down the walls of Jericho, I hear and see the walls falling, I hear the prisons walls shaking, I hear the chains falling down. The prisoners are free. The wall of Jericho has collapsed, I see young leaders rising up and breaking down all the evil influences of the world. I decree and declare that the walls are falling down. I truly believe that this generation will step up, an army of youth and young adults.

In Acts 2:17-18 "In the last days, God says, I will pour out my Spirit on all people. Your sons and daughters will prophesy, your young men will see visions, your old men will dream dreams. Even on my servants, both men and women, I will pour out my Spirit in those days, and they will prophesy."

In 1 Timothy 4:10-16 "In fact this is why we work hard and struggle, because we have set our hope on the living God, who is the Savior of all people, especially of believers.

Command and teach these things. Let no one look down on you because you are young, but set an example for the believers in your speech, conduct, love, faithfulness, and purity. Until I come, give attention to the public reading of scripture, to exhortation, to teaching. Do not neglect the spiritual gift you have, given to you and confirmed by prophetic words when the elders laid hands on you.

Take pains with these things; be absorbed in them, so that everyone will see your progress. Be conscientious about how you live and what you teach. Persevere in this, because by doing so you will save both yourself and those who listen to you."

There is an army of God rising up in the youth and young adults to break all the curses and chains of the enemy. These young people are bold and are not afraid of using the word of God to defeat the enemy. In fact, these young people are willing to give up their lives to fight for Jesus Christ and save all the lost souls of the world. All these young people are One Body Risen in Christ and look just like God because they are God's Army. God is calling more people younger every day because they are more bold, obedient and willing to give up their lives to follow Jesus Christ.

There is power in the name of Jesus. This power is from the Army of God of young people across the globe of all nations, race, gender, and backgrounds. These young people are spread across nations speaking about the world of God, healing all kinds of incurable disease, giving the blind sight, making the deaf hear, bringing the dead back to life, making the poor rich, restoring lives, restoring marriages, restoring families, erasing/canceling debts, giving away keys to new houses/cars that is already paid for, and rising up more prophets, apostles, and evangelists to fulfill God's purpose for their lives. Our Lord is raising up youth leaders so the Glory of God will shine through them. So the young leaders will walk fully with the resurrection of Jesus Christ so we will be made new, fully and abundantly.

It's not even about church anymore; these young people are one body in Christ in the Church. It is about the head of the church, Jesus Christ, whispering to the youth, ARISE to those who have ears to hear and hearts ready to obey.

Woman Of God: Who Did God Create You to Be?

In Isaiah 60:1-2 1 "Arise! Shine! For your light arrives! The splendor of the Lord shines on you! For, look, darkness covers the earth and deep darkness cover the nations, but the Lord shines on you; his splendor appears over you."

Are you going to join these young people and be a part of the army of God or get left behind? I know I am still young myself at just 26 years old but I am a part of God's Army! Now the walls are broken, the chains have fallen down so it's up to you to obey or not!

Woman Of God: Who Did God Create You to Be?

Are you going to say "Yes" to God?

All you have to do is open your mouth and say yes. I will do whatever you want me to, God I will say whatever you want me to say. I am nothing without you, there is no other option but you so all I can say is Yes Lord let your will be done in me. Have your way with me, I tried my way and it didn't work. Everyone has turned their backs on my family and me disowns me. In fact, I no longer recognize myself anymore. "Who am I?"

I'm tired of sleepless nights and waking up with strangers in my bed. Jesus Christ, I cry out to you take away these heartaches and pains from me. Lord, I'm down on my knees asking for a deliverance of drugs and alcohol. Take away the taste of drugs, alcohol, crack, cocaine, Cigarettes and foul language out my mouth.

I surrender to your will, I'm walking away from this crack house, guide me along the way. Jesus Christ says "I have always been there waiting for you to come out on your own and I have been guiding a righteous way for you all along but I was waiting until you said Yes Lord I am ready!"

"Lord I am ready, my heart, soul and spirit Say Yes. I cannot do this alone without you my Heavenly Father! You have protected me when no one else was there, you kept me covered by the blood of your precious son Jesus Christ and you kept me safe from getting HIV/AIDS, Genital Herpes or any other form of STDS!

God said "Yes my child come out, I'm calling you out your dry bones and I am calling you higher because I have so much more that I require of you! I don't care what the world think or say you are my child. No man can do my will but me, no man can work it out but me so come out that wilderness and do my will for your life, my child. I love you so much and I have been waiting for you for a very long time. I forgave you for your sins of your past and I called you to rule many nations just like I promise Abraham, Isaac and Jacob!"

Tears are running down my eyes and all I can say is Yes Father, I come to you. I love you too. I see your face, I hear your voice, I feel your presence and I know you are with me so I have no choice but to trust you. My God you are so awesome, you made miracles happen for even people like me, and you have pulled me out that crack house when others were afraid to go in that you were there even when I was at my lowest point so at this time I made up my mind. I praise and worship, all I can do is Say Yes Lord, I am not afraid I will stand by the Glory and favor of God. I will spread your word and do your will to all nations. Lord, I thank you for the healing and deliverance!

In Ezekiel 2:4-7: "The people to whom I am sending you are obstinate and hard-hearted and you must say to them, 'This is what the sovereign Lord says.' And as for them, whether they listen or not – for they are a rebellious house – they will know that a prophet has been among them. But you, son of man, do not fear them, and do not fear their words – even though briers and thorns surround you and you live among scorpions – do not fear their words and do not be terrified of the looks they give you, for they are a rebellious house! You must speak my words to them whether they listen or not, for they are rebellious."

In Ezekiel 37:4-10 "Then he said to me, "Prophesy over these bones, and tell them: 'Dry bones, hear the word of the Lord. 5 This is what the sovereign Lord says to these bones: Look, I am about to infuse breath into you and you will live.6 I will put tendons on you and muscles over you and will cover you with skin; I will put breath in you and you will live. Then you will know that I am the Lord.'" 7 So I prophesied as I was commanded. There was a sound when I prophesied – I heard a rattling, and the bones came together, bone to bone. 8 As I watched, I saw tendons on them, then muscles appeared, and skin covered over them from above, but there was no breath in them. 9 He said to me, "Prophesy to the breath, – prophesy, son of man – and say to the breath: 'this is what the sovereign Lord says: Come from the four winds, O breath, and breathe on these corpses so that they may live."

    My Child I am calling you higher, I cannot do my will without you being ready so yes my child come out that dry place and be that woman that I created you to be! Look at me My Child, See my face, hear my voice, I'm calling you higher, and I have an uncommon predestination purpose on your life. The day you heard my voice harden not your heart and Say Yes. There is so much more I require of you! My Child let your heart, soul and spirit Say Yes Lord!

The World Will Hate You

When you are a follower of Christ, the world will hate you regardless of how nice and kind you are. They will hate you because the more time you spend with Jesus Christ, the more you will become like him. God will give you a prophet like him, who is one of your own people. This prophet can be a man or woman but he/she will teach you everything you need to know, so you can go out and help others in all nations. However, all people will not accept you, especially your family; they will be the hardest one and will hate you the most. Now you know for a fact that your family will not accept you as a prophet but you know what you are. God already made you a prophet, apostle, evangelist or pastor before you were in your mother's womb and you cannot change that. If you do not accept that title, God will put you in a position where you have no choice but to accept that title.

In Luke 21:16-17 "And ye shall be betrayed both by parents, and brethren, and kinsfolk's, and friends; and some of you shall they cause to be put to death. And ye shall be hated of all men for my name's sake."

Your family is the worst ones and will hurt you the most. It might hurt you but it is the truth. Remember the world hated Jesus Christ before they hate you. People will leave out your lives, you can't change them so let them go. They are not meant to be in your life in the first place. Do not try to change anything; you keep your eyes on Christ. Everyone can't go where you are going because it is not meant for them to go with you.

In Acts 7:51-53 "You stubborn people, with uncircumcised hearts and ears! You are always resisting the Holy Spirit like your ancestors did! Which of the prophets did your ancestors not persecute? They killed those who foretold long ago the coming of the Righteous One, whose betrayers and murderers you have now become! You received the law by decrees given by angels, but you did not obey it."

I know I went through Hell with my family, they turned completely against me. What makes it so sad was that I lived with them? They will call me so many negative names and everything but my name. In fact, one day they called me stupid and crazy because I always said that God will work out everything. I just stop talking to them about God because they will never understand. That day I learned you can't always talk to people about God tell them what God said because they won't receive it. Even though some of my family members turned against me, not all of them did and I became closer to other members of my family and brought them closer to Jesus Christ.

What I had to realize is that I had to follow God regardless of the situation? My family couldn't take me where Jesus Christ could so I kept falling God, even more, I didn't care about my family getting mad at me. The more I became closer to Jesus Christ the more they hate me because they said I was changing and I did not act the same anymore. The enemy had them so blind and fooled they could not see I changed for the better. Therefore, they were looking, hearing and seeing with their natural eyes instead of with their spiritual eyes and ears.

During my journey walk with God I have lost so many so called friends, family members, and other people as well but God will remove people out your life for a reason. I had to learn that God will separate you from people that will hinder your walk with Jesus Christ and through it all it will make you stronger. God will use provokers to promote you!

Sow A Seed

A lot of people do not understand what it means to sow a seed. What that person fails to realize is that you are really sowing to the Kingdom of God? Yes, I know that pastor has more than three churches and riding around in Bentleys and other fancy cars. Men and women of God, your focus should be on Christ instead of try to figure out whether that person is real or not. Did you know that you are not sowing into a man but the kingdom of God? It doesn't matter if that person is real or not you just do what God told you to do. Every time you turn on the television someone is talking about sowing seed. However, that so-called pastor will suffer in the end, not you because you have to realize God created everything in this world, not people. God is the creator and owns everything.

Now I know you are wondering how do you sow a seed? Let me beginning by telling you my testimonials and others: I remember one Wednesday night I was at church; I didn't even have gas in my car. All I remember is God telling me to put my last 10 dollars in church, let me remind you I did not have a job. Do you know I obeyed the Holy Spirit, God lead me home without running out of gas but it's even better because that Friday afternoon someone western union me 100 dollars, but this person never gave me any money before. It gets better because one Sunday morning God told me to put 15 dollars in church and He even told me what to wear that morning. I obeyed the Holy Spirit again; however, that Monday something happens that was different someone gave me 320 dollars but it gets even better because that Wednesday evening someone else gave me 300 more dollars. I know it might seem like it's not a lot of money but trust me when you don't have anything it's a lot to you.

Woman Of God: Who Did God Create You to Be?

Do you know God did that for me and I didn't even have to ask or beg anyone for money? There was this woman at my church, she didn't even have a job, and all she had was 22 dollars in her purse. She gave that last 22 dollars and the next day, she received a job that pays 22 dollars an hour. It was even people at my church that were getting large amounts of money from unfamiliar places but God knew it was there all alone. One woman receives an 18,000 dollar check for a down payment of any car of her choice. One couple even receives a check for 11,000 dollars.

Others were getting checks and money for all sources. There was also this one couple who lost their job, now the wife did not work but they had faith in God. The husband receives unemployed checks, it was 200 and something dollars. If you see this couple today, you will never realize they were broke and didn't have anything. They have over 3 houses and many expensive cars now. In Luke 21:3-4 "He said, I tell you the truth, this poor widow woman gave more than all those rich people. They gave only what they did not need. This woman is very poor, but she gave all she had to live on." It doesn't matter what you give, it's where your heart is when you give. God will turn a 10 dollar seed and multiply it.

Don't tell me what God can't do, because you can get paid by working for God and He provides for your every need. I don't care if you believe me or not but I know what I went through and what God did for me. Yes God will take you through seasons where you don't have anyone to work for but God. I remember I would apply to jobs like crazy but no one will hire me, I would go on interviews but no one will hire me. Eventually, I grew tired and frustrated so that night I asked God why I couldn't get a job! That same night I had a dream, God told me to trust him to provide for me, no matter where I went to apply for a job no one is going to hire you, Christy, because I want you to trust me to provide for you and your son?

If I haven't had that dream that night, I would have never understood by working for God. Let me remind you I lived in an 800 dollars apartment, my son's tuition feed were 545 a month but God made a way for my rent and son's tuition to get paid every month. Now I didn't get government assistance either, we still had food, lights, cable, clothes, shoes and everything. We always had more than what we needed. However, I do love to be a fashionable dress, how about I and my son had expensive clothes and shoes to wear that were brand new.

I don't know if you read about what I wrote about not having a job, but its gets even greater because God made a way so I could get an apartment, with no job, no co-signer, no check studs or nothing. How about that same year in 2020, I moved into my apartment? God made a way so I could get a brand new 2010 SS Camero that looks like the one in the movie Transforms with no job, no driver's license, no checks studs, no insurance, no co-signer or nothing. It was the exact car I wanted but I just wanted a regular Camero, but God had something greater for me. Everything was paid for that day; I never had a car note a day in my life.

God sends His blessings through people, what one man won't do; God will send someone else to do it for him. Jesus Christ died on the cross for our sins so we can be like him and be closer to our Heavenly Father again. He left us with the Holy Spirit to guide us.

Now, this goes back to my question "How do you sow a seed?" Men and women of God, I know sometimes you don't have money to put in the basket but if you have a

Woman Of God: Who Did God Create You to Be?

penny give it to God because it's about where your heart is when you give. Sometimes you might be in situations where you don't have any money to give but give what you have. Did you know sowing seeds does not always have to be money? If you just have that enveloped in your hands give that to God and just write Yes Lord I trust you. It's about your heart when you give.

There was this one boy that was 15 years old, all he had was his iPhone, he put that same iPhone in the basket, the next day he receive 3 brand new phones that were newer versions of that old iPhone, all the phones were working too. There were days where my church had clothing drives and I will give away my expensive clothes that were brand new and still had price tags on them. When you give, give with your heart.

Oh don't let me forget, there was this one time I gave a small cross necklace to the Kingdom of God that someone gave me as a gift for my birthday. A couple of days later I look on my dresser and I saw the most beautiful necklace and earrings set from Kay jeweler. It shocked me because I haven't seen that same necklace or earrings in almost 3 years. It was very special to me because my son's father had bought it for me as a gift 3 years earlier. Let me remind you my son's father is not around anymore because God separated us for a season. In fact, when I saw that necklace and earrings I realize that my son's father was going through a lot and he didn't mean to leave us. God let me know that my son's father still loved us and miss us more every day. That same day I forgave my son's father for leaving us and it gave me peace with him. Now I still pray for his deliverance and my son pray for him as well but I know eventually he will be that Godly Father to my son that God called him to be.

Woman Of God: Who Did God Create You to Be?

People might think or might not understand by working for God but some people might think you are even stupid or crazy, always trust God and give with your heart. The job will come in the right season because while you're jobless, God will teach you things to help others. Think about it, if you work all time, you will always be too busy or not have enough time for God so God will put you in situations where you have no choice but to reply on Him. God even have something greater for you because while you're looking for a job, God is trying to make you into the CEO. In Deuteronomy 28:13 "And the LORD shall make thee the head, and not the tail; and thou shalt be above only, and thou shalt not be beneath; if that thou hearken unto the commandments of the LORD thy God, which I command thee this day, to observe and to do them."

Women of God sow what God tells you to do, give with your heart regardless of what that so-called pastor asks for. I know I was at a church, every Sunday my so called pastor at that time always ask for a 100 or more for every program they had. I used to feel bad because I didn't have any money to give. But I left that church and learn about giving to the Kingdom of God, I learn and understand everything so much better now. No one knew what I went through because the Glory of God will shine right through me and I did not look like what I was going through. To this day, no one knew until I told my story to others now. I pray that you all give what you have and sow into the Kingdom of God because He will bless you with so much more.

You're a Lost Child on the Inside

I see right through you, you're so lost and confused on the inside. You're a grown man/woman and you can't even think for yourself. You have lost your identity and you do not recognize yourself anymore. You don't know how to be yourself because you want to fit in, being like everyone else and please people instead of God. You're afraid to change because if you do, your so-called friends won't come around anymore. This child is so lost because he/she does not realize that these people are not really their friends. In reality, those people envy you and are jealous of you because they can see the God in you and they know God has something greater in your life. These people will do anything in their power to keep you from doing what God called you to do.

You drink, smoke, do drugs, have random sex partners, party all night, go to clubs to make people happy but deep down inside you know that person is not really you and you know you don't belong there. You chase these men/women that you know are not good for you, you know they are using you to get what they want and all they see is dollar signs. Therefore, you settle because you are not ready for a real man/woman. When you meet that real woman/man, you run or hurt that person because that same person is changing you and making you into that person God called you to be.

Even though it hurts you deep down inside, you love and miss that same man/woman you hurt, but you feel like it's too late to change and fix that relationship. You know that woman/man was telling you the truth all along but you refused to listen. Instead of working on getting better, you become even more vulnerable and depressed. You don't know how to control your emotions so you go

Woman Of God: Who Did God Create You to Be?

right back to the things you know and feel more comfortable with. However, you meet someone else but it's not the same because you're still in love with the person you hurt.

It's not going to work because you tried to replace that man/woman you hurt but that other person is hurting you and damaging you on the inside. It's too late to change because you don't want to admit that you were wrong and you hurt that other person for no reason.

It hurts you so bad and it's killing you on the inside but your so called friends are still in your ear, saying that man/woman won't even have sex with you. He/she doesn't love you, that person won't even spend the night with you. That man/woman is trying to change you; you don't even act the same anymore. She/he thinks they are better than you, they see you as trash and their family doesn't even like you. What you fell to realize is that regardless of what that man/woman family thinks they still love you because they see the real person inside of you and they know God is in you! This man/woman loves you so much and is praying for your deliverance when no one else is praying for you or when you even gave up on yourself but you have to realize that yourself.

Also, what your so called friends don't know is that you cry at night and some nights you can't sleep because you miss that same man/woman you hurt! Everything you do will remind you of that person, it's hurts you because you can't talk to that man/woman. All you want to do is hear their voice or see that man/woman beautiful face again but you can't because your so called friends will be mad at you. While you're crying and missing that man/woman, God will use that same man/woman you hurt to pray for you at 1, 2 or 3 o' clock in the morning. In fact, God will wake up these men/women of God at certain times to pray for you because they can feel you thinking about them and no one else is praying for you.

Oh, lost child let me tell you a little secret; your so called friends don't care about you. In fact, they are jealous of what you have and hate to see you happy. Your so called friends want to be you and want your lifestyle. The so called friends know you are changing for the better and getting closer to Christ. Therefore, the so called friends want what you have; they want someone like that same man/woman you hurt. In fact, I wouldn't be surprised if the so called friends will try to get with that same man/woman you hurt.

You are who you surround yourselves around, so watch those so called friends; they are snakes and will bite you in the end.

In the end, all your so called friends will walk out your lives and leave you with nothing. All these men/women you chase that mean you no good will leave you shameless and nothing else left. Everyone will walk right out your life but that same man/woman that you hurt will be standing there waiting for you.

God loves you so much and He will meet you right where you are. It doesn't matter what you have done, God forgave you for your past. Jesus Christ loves you so much, he will put people in your life to change you and become like our savior Jesus Christ. As a result that is where that same man/woman you hurt gets their strength from the grace of God and God gives them the strength for you to be strong when you can't even be strong for yourself. Trust me that same man/woman could have easy walked away, they deserve someone so much better but God keeps telling that same person that you love them and you didn't mean to hurt them. It takes a strong man/woman of God to go through all that hurt, heartache, pain but to still love that person that hurt them and to have a forgiving heart.

    Oh, lost child you must love God and yourself before you love anyone else! How can you love someone when you don't even love yourself? Stop being a lost child and stop filling those voids with things that you know is hurting and damaging your body. The only person you need to chase is Jesus Christ, ask for forgiveness and God will bring that same man/woman you hurt back to you but you must be right with Jesus Christ first. God will not allow you to be with that man/woman of God and you are corrupt. That's why it seems like that person left you but in reality, God separates you two so you can be like God and stop sinning.

    Each time you two separate God will bring both of you closer to Christ, you might not understand it but God knows what He is doing. What God joints together, let no man separate but trust me don't wait too long. If it's taking you too long to change, He will send someone else to take your place and be that Godly husband/wife to that same person you hurt. So lost child I suggest that you change your wicked ways, stop listening to the so-called friends and be the men/women that God called you to be before you end of losing your one true love. You will never find anyone else like that man/woman you hurt but change for yourself, don't do it for that man/woman you hurt. Do it for yourself and God, always keep God first and He will work out everything else for you! It is truly a gift from God to have found your soul mate so don't let that person walk away from you, you do everything in your power to make it work!

Keep Your Faith

If you have faith over a few things, you will rule over many! No matter what you're going through in life, you have to keep believing in God. There were many days I cried, words come not even come out my mouth, all I could say was Lord I thank you! Tears will run down my eyes and I didn't even know why but I had to trust God. It wasn't another option for me because I had no one else left.

God remove everyone out my life, my so called friends, my family turned against me. In fact, the closer I will get to God, the more they hated me. In Luke 21:16:17 "Even your parents, brothers, relatives, and friends will turn against you, and they will kill some of you. All people will hate you because you follow me." It was just so much going on, I didn't even understand it but I keep saying, God, I trust you; let your will be done in my life.

Sometimes it will be so over bearing I will be like why God? His response was "Everything you're going through Christy is to make you stronger because I have an uncommon purpose for your life. I gave you the faith of Abraham because you are my chosen one and you're the only one in your family that can handle it. No one is strong like you are, even though you walk through the valley of the shadow of death, you've kept your faith."

Faith moves mountains. You have to have outrageous faith regardless of what you're going through. Jesus Christ said all you need is faith as small as a mustard seed and you will get anything you ask for, all you have to do is ask and believe.

No matter how hard it might get, I don't care if you lost your job, trust God because He has something better for you. I don't care if you lost your car, home or lost everything you had, trust God even more. God still has something greater for you. You're going to have trials and tribulations along the way but keep your faith.

God will use a homeless man in street before He will use a rich man because that homeless man is humble and is more willing to go to unfamiliar places to preach the word of God. God will use a person that people will see as a nothing and rise that person up higher and people wouldn't know, that same man or woman was homeless, depressed, almost killed themselves, abused, and on drugs and alcohol. These people won't look like what they went through because the Glory of God will shine through them.

Whatever one person won't do, God will rise up someone else to do it for him. Have you notice that God is using younger people than the older people now? What one generation won't do, God will rise a generation that are willing to lose their lives for our savior Jesus Christ. At the end, God will bless you even more so you must keep your faith and do not give up!

Spiritual Battle

Have you ever been around a person and you feel nothing but negative energy? Whenever this person comes around, you feel a strong presence and you can't be around that person long. In fact, you do everything in your power to stay away from that person. This person makes you feel so uncomfortable and you can feel all the negative energy pulling on your spirit. The only thing you keep thinking is that I have to get away from this person, you dislike seeing this person coming towards your way so you try your best to avoid them.

Every word that comes out that person's mouth is negative or violent. Every time you see that person, they're gossiping and talking bad about someone else. They always use fool language when they speak and plot evil things against God's people because they envy them.

This person is always fighting, arguing, hurting and discouraging others. This person has multiple evil spirits. No one likes this person. This person is also a liar and a cheater.

In fact, this person is not a real person because it is not what you see with your natural eyes, you can only see the real person with your spiritual eyes. When you have a personal relationship with God, you're truly one of God's people; however, this person will reveal its true identity to you.

Many may ask "Who is this person?" This person is no one other than Lucifer himself. In John 10:10 "The thief cometh not, but for to steal, and to kill, and to destroy." In Micah 7:6 "For the son dishonoureth the father, the daughter riseth up against her mother, the daughter in law against her mother in law; a man's enemies are the men of his own house." The enemy does everything in his power to destroy God's people.

Men and women of God what you have to understand is that we are not dealing with people; we are dealing with evil spirits. We are in a spiritual battle so you can't get mad at the evil things others plot against you. These people are not who they say they are and they are lost themselves. They discourage others to make themselves feel better; they are bitter and unhappy on the inside.

When you find yourselves around that type of person, do not try to get even with them. You can't fight against evil spirits but God can through your prayers and fasting. The best thing you can do is to pray for that person to be delivering from their evil ways. There is even a time when you can pray against evil spirits because, at the midnight hour, Lucifer uses his evil spirits to attack God's people. It starts from 12 midnight until 3 a.m. Let's not forget that God has his prayer warriors too and God's people are praying for all of God's children that cannot pray for themselves. It is someone praying for you right now and you don't even know that person.

Men and women of God again I say to you is to realize that you are not dealing with people; we're in a spiritual battle. Instead of disliking that person, pray for them because we need more prayer warriors and we need to rise up an army of prophets, apostles, and evangelisms.

Woman Of God: Who Did God Create You to Be?

Jezebel's Spirit

This woman was known as the wickedest woman the world and she loved power. She is the most evil spirit in the bible and she is still in this world today. Her name Jezebel means a morally corrupt woman. So this woman was very proud of her pride.

In fact, she did everything evil in the sight of God. She grew up a worshiper of Baal and she did witchcraft. She tried everything she could to keep the people from worshiping God and turning them against God. In 1 Kings 18:4 "For it was so, when Jezebel cut off the prophets of the LORD, that Obadiah took a hundred prophets, and hid them by fifty in a cave, and fed them with bread and water.)"

God even send his prophet Elijah to save Israel and to change the heart of Jezebel. However, she was too far gone and could not be saved. In 1 Kings 18:18, Elijah said: "And he answered, I have not troubled Israel; but thou, and thy father's house, in that ye have forsaken the commandments of the LORD, and thou hast followed, Baal."

Jezebel did everything that was evil including sexual immorality, prostitution, and even sacrifices children. It gets even crazier because this woman was also a false prophet but claimed to be a woman of God.

In 1 Kings 21:23 "And of Jezebel also spake the LORD, saying, The dogs shall eat Jezebel by the wall of Jezreel." In 2 Kings 9:36-37 "Wherefore they came again and told him. And he said, This is the word of the LORD, which he spake by his servant Elijah the Tishbite, saying, In the portion of Jezreel shall dogs eat the flesh of Jezebel:

Woman Of God: Who Did God Create You to Be?

And the carcase of Jezebel shall be as dung upon the face of the field in the portion of Jezreel; so that they shall not say, This is Jezebel." God cursed Jezebel in the end and she suffers greatly.

Why do I say Jezebel's spirit still roams through the Earth today? Jezebel roams the Earth to find lost and vulnerable women so she can attack them. These women have low self-esteem and will do anything to get attention by the way they dress, act and the way they carry themselves. These women have no respect for themselves or others. It is so many women that have this spirit and do not even know it. It is sad because people are not even aware of the Jezebel spirit or know she still existence today. When women have sex with different men, it's her spirit. Women do not know it because they believe they are having fun and enjoying life. Then they will be in church on Sunday mornings praising God. What they don't realize is that Jezebel is using their bodies until no one wants them anymore.

Women who like to dominate men have that evil spirit. Many women use their beauty to get what they want but they don't know it's that old Jezebel spirit inside of them. When women become prostitutes and strippers they are lost, confused; however, they do not know the Jezebel spirit took over their lives.

Women of God take control of your lives, be aware of that sneaky, evil, conniving, nasty, and disguising Jezebel spirit!

The Fire of God

In Genesis 22:2 "And he said, Take now thy son, thine only son Isaac, whom thou lovest, and get thee into the land of Moriah; and offer him there for a burnt-offering upon one of the mountains which I will tell thee of." God told Abraham to sacrifice his only son Isaac, which God promise Abraham that nations will be blessed through Isaac.

In Genesis 22:6 "And Abraham took the wood of the burnt-offering, and laid it upon Isaac, his son, and he took the fire in his hand, and a knife; and they went both of them together." When Abraham went to the mountaintop, he was carrying the fire with him. No one can carry the fire but God but in the bible, it says that Abraham was carrying the fire in his hand.

In Hebrew 11:17-19: "By faith Abraham, when he was tried, offered up Isaac: and he that had received the promises offered up his only begotten son, 18 Of whom it was said, That in Isaac shall thy seed be called: 19 Accounting that God was able to raise him up, even from the dead; from whence also he received him in a figure."

Abraham was carrying the fire of God in his hand and He also believes that God will raise Isaac from the dead when no one has even heard of resurrection yet. This was in Abraham's time and Jesus Christ hasn't come yet. Therefore, people what I'm saying is that Abraham's was just like God, no one could have thought like that but a man just like God. In fact, Abraham's faith was so strong he thought exactly the way God does.

However, because of Abraham's obedience, his offspring Isaac ruled many nations through him. In Genesis

Woman Of God: Who Did God Create You to Be?

22:12-13 "And he said, Lay not thine hand upon the lad, neither do thou anything unto him: for now I know that thou fearest God, seeing thou hast not withheld thy son, thine only son from me.13 And Abraham lifted up his eyes, and looked, and behold behind him a ram caught in a thicket by his horns: and Abraham went and took the ram, and offered him up for a burnt-offering in the stead of his son." In Genesis 22:17-18 "That in blessing I will bless thee, and in multiplying I will multiply thy seed as the stars of the heaven, and as the sand which is upon the sea-shore; and thy seed shall possess the gate of his enemies; 18 And in thy seed shall all the nations of the earth be blessed; because thou hast obeyed my voice."

Men and women of God no matter what you are going through in life, you must be willing to carry the fire of God. It doesn't matter what people say or think about you, you have to keep your faith and trust, God. If you're not in your manifestation season yet, still trust God and be willing to carry the fire with you. When you're in unfamiliar places or situations, that's when you have to trust The Lord the most because He has a happy ending for you.

It doesn't matter if you're alone, no one wants to carry the fire with you; however, you must be willing to carry the fire alone and know that God is right there with you.

People will have to make sacrifices to carry the fire of God because everyone is not meant to go with them. When you're carrying the fire, you leave everything behind including family members or so-called friends. God will supply your every need along the way. When you're carrying the fire, you will have to be exactly like God. When you're going through things, you don't even understand why you carry the fire with you. If you lost everything you have, you're at your lowest point with tears in your eyes you still willing to carry the fire of God with you. No matter what circumstances you're in still be willing to carry the fire of God with you because God has something so much greater for you and He has an uncommon predestination for your life. Men and women of God be like Abraham and carry the fire when God has you to do something that may be strange to you but carry the fire of God in your hand trust God and keep your faith!

Kingdom of God

Did you know you can live in the kingdom of God on Earth? In Matthew 6:9-10: "Our Father, which art in heaven, Hallowed be thy name. 10 Thy kingdom come. Thy will be done in earth, as it is in heaven."

Did you know you can become so intimate with God that your prayers will open the gates of Heaven? You may ask "How can I do that?"

It's actually simple, the more time you spend with God, the more you become like Christ. It is more than just reading your bible or going to church. You have to stop sinning and completely obey our Lord. People you will have to change the way you think and start thinking like Jesus Christ. You will have to see things the way God does, hear, smell, feel and even taste things the way God does. Therefore, people you will have to be just like Jesus Christ and people will see the Glory of God shining through you.

In John 14:12-14 "Verily, verily, I say unto you, He that believeth on me, the works that I do shall he do also; and greater works than these shall he do; because I go unto my Father. 13 And whatsoever ye shall ask in my name, that will I do, that the Father may be glorified in the Son. 14 If ye shall ask any thing in my name, I will do it." Jesus Christ said you can do the same things I do; all you have to do is just ask.

You can become so much like Christ, your prayers will open the gates of Heaven and you will be living in the Kingdom of God. Whatever you ask for God will give it to you because He can trust you with His true wisdom and wealth.

Woman Of God: Who Did God Create You to Be?

God loves us, he wants us to live in wealth but we have to come to him first. God did create us to live poverty. In 2 Corinthians 8:9 "For ye know the grace of our Lord Jesus Christ, that, though he was rich, yet for your sakes he became poor, that ye through his poverty might be rich. "Jesus Christ was poor so we can become rich.

When God created us, he already made millionaire and billionaire potential inside of us; it's up to us to find it. Therefore, people you chose your own destiny in life, it's already inside of us. God did not make you without a purpose for him. We chose to live the Kingdom of God or not, but you can't do it with sinning. People if I were you I would choose to live in the Kingdom of God!

What is Wealth?

Is wealth silver or gold? Riches or wealth is in your heart. What do you do when you have nothing left inside of you? Do you cry or look to the sky for answers? How much struggle can you take? Can you handle the pain that Jesus Christ took on the cross for our sins?

No, I don't think so because Jesus Christ pain was ten times worst! So struggle has nothing over you but you must struggle before you reach your wealth zones.

When I dream, I make my dreams into reality on Earth. I dream that God was pouring down gold into my life and it was Gold all around me, it surrounds me everywhere I went. Gold is my wealth. Gold represents the divine nature. As gold is the highest, most precious metal, so the divine nature is the highest nature, the only nature having immortality. The color Gold reflects a spiritual reward, richness, refinement and enhancement of your surroundings. It also signifies your determination and unyielding nature.

The only thing I can say about this dream is that I believe God; I have faith that all things are possible through God. I believe and I receive! In Psalm 21:3 "For you meet him with rich blessings; you set a crown of fine gold upon his head."

Do you believe God will pour down silver or gold in your life? Well, I believe in the power of God. I will live in the Kingdom of God and Kingdom Of Heaven on Earth. So are you ready to receive your wealth of gold pouring down in your life? In Ezekiel 28:4 "By your wisdom and your understanding you have made wealth for yourself and have gathered gold and silver into your treasuries."

Just Be Yourself

When God created you, He made you stand out from everyone else. God made you unique individuals. Why are you trying to fit in and please everyone else when you know you don't belong there? Why are you're clubbing, smoking, drinking and doing drugs? Those things will not fulfill that empty void that is inside of you. Why are you having sex with strangers, when you know they don't value you? You know they are out to harm you but you want to be popular and follow the in crowd.

Oh wait but you want to be just like Beyoncé, Kim Kardashian and Nicki Minja so you idol them, then they become your God. It's so sad because the young men want to be like the rappers Lil Wayne, Rich Homie Quan and Future. I'm not saying they are bad people but the only person you should idol and strive to be like is Jesus Christ. Young people stop trying to live and be like the celebrities. We need more apostles, prophets, and evangelists in this world today. The world has enough doctors and lawyers but we need more people who are not afraid to spread the gospel to all nations and not afraid to be themselves.

In this generation in this society today is a generation curse of non-believers and money hungry people. Money is the root of all evil. In 1 Timothy 6:10 "For the love of money is the root of all evil: which while some coveted after, they have erred from the faith, and pierced themselves through with many sorrows." God says whoever loves money more than you love me shall perish and have a life of pain and sorrows because they lost faith in God.

Our society of young men and women minds are so conquered and damage because they listen to celebrities instead of God. I pray for this young generation because of what they hear and see on television and the internet. These celebrities make it seem like it's okay to have sex with random people they don't even know, to smoke, to do drugs and alcohol. However, homosexuality is more open than it ever was before, marriages are decreasing and the divorce rate is higher than it ever was. God said these are all sins so people pray for forgiveness and repentance. (Not all celebrities are bad but young people follow the ones who are negative influence the most because they feel they are more powerful).

Stop being afraid to be who God created you to be. If you surround yourselves around more positive influence people, you will be like Jesus Christ. You are who you surround yourselves around.

People find out what your purpose is in life, we need more people to be themselves, stop trying to live like the world. When God created us, He made all of us for reason, be yourself and walk into your purpose for God. In fact, your true wealth comes from your true purpose for God. Whatever you're called to do it must line up with the word of God, bring many people to Jesus Christ as you can and to save all the lost souls.

Why settle to be an Ishmael when God made you an Isaac? You are Abraham's seed and Abraham's seed ruled many nations!

Traditions and Religious

Tradition is the transmission of customs or beliefs from generation to generation or the fact of being passed on in this way. It is passing down of elements of a culture from generation to generation, especially by oral communication.

Religious is the belief in and worship of a superhuman controlling power, especially a personal God or gods. A set of beliefs concerning the cause, nature, and purpose of the universe, especially when considered as the creation of a superhuman agency or agencies, usually involving devotional and ritual observances, and often containing a moral code governing the conduct of human affairs.

People are so stuck in traditions and religious that they can't prosper into what God called them to do. They are so afraid to step outside the norm and so worried about what people think about them. People will stay at their same dead church just because their family grew up in that church from one generation to the next generation. (In fact, people are more focus on the church than God. It's not even in the bible that tells you how a church supposed to look.) They are afraid to try different churches that are led by the Holy Spirit because it's new to them and they never experienced anything like that before.

Therefore, people are so stuck in traditions and religious that they don't believe in women pastors, apostles, and prophets but majority of them do not even go to church. What kind of God are you serving? It can't be the one God that created us in his very own image or whose son Jesus Christ died for our sins. In Galatians 3:28 "There is neither Jew nor Greek, there is neither bond nor free, there is neither male nor female: for ye are all one in Christ Jesus." God can use anyone to spread his word to all nations because He does not see gender and we all are one in Jesus Christ.

However, people love to bring up these two bible scriptures 1 Corinthians 14:34-35:34 "Let your women keep silence in the churches: for it is not permitted unto them to speak; but they are commanded to be under obedience, as also saith the law. 35 And if they will learn anything, let them ask their husbands at home: for it is a shame for women to speak in the church." 11 Let the woman learn in silence with all subjection. 1 Timothy 11:12: 11 Let the woman learn in silence with all subjection. 12 But I suffer not a woman to teach, nor to usurp authority over the man, but to be in silence.

Before I speak about this subject, let me say this person when you read your bibles you have to be led by the Holy Spirit instead of reading it like a book. Ask God to give you the Holy Spirit so you can understand what you are reading.

When Paul wrote that he did not say women cannot be pastors. For one reason Paul is not God and God said before you believe anything you should always ask him first. Paul wrote that because the church needed order because they were out of order. The church was in destruction after Paul left and they were sinning and doing things the wrong way. In 1 Corinthians 14:40 "Let all things be done decently and in order."

Now Timothy wrote that for the married couples, he did not want the husband's wives to over speak them and make an embarrassment of themselves. It was a lot of issues with women in the churches because they did not know how to act property and act like First Ladies in the churches! He did not say women could not be pastors; he was talking about the men wives who were not a part of the ministry. He wanted the women to have order in the church!

Now another reason people don't believe in women pastors, apostles, and prophets is because they are ignorant. The devil will have people so ignorant and they don't even realize they are ignorant. In fact, that's why many people are so stuck in traditions and religious. In 1 Corinthians 14:38 "But if any man be ignorant, let him be ignorant." In fact, ignorance is one of the main attacks that the enemy will use against people to keep them from doing what God called them to do. If the enemy will use you with ignorance he will because he already knows what God called you to do so he stops it with ignorance before it happens and people fail to realize it all the time.

People I plead the blood of Jesus over you, open up your eyes and walk into God promise land. God may move you away from your family to a new church, city, and state or move you away from your so called friends, but just trust God because He knows what's best for you. It may be too strange to others but who cares what people think. If you follow others, you will be stuck in traditions and religious like they are. I decree and declare that you will walk out on faith and follow Jesus. It doesn't matter who gets left behind as long as it is not you.

Do not worry about anything because God will supply your every need. He might put you in unfamiliar places or unfamiliar situations but just trust God through it all because He has an uncommon purpose on your life.

Prayer and Fasting

Prayer is the most important part of our daily lives. If you do not pray, you are not a part of God kingdom. Prayer changes things and situations in the atmosphere of our lives. When you pray, you can even make your enemies bow down to the name of Jesus. Prayer can make the impossible come into reality. In fact, the more you pray, the more you become the image of God and through prayer you speak things into existence. Therefore, prayer can also help you to listen and hear God's voice more. In fact, the more you pray, your prayers will open up the gates of Heaven.

However, I know many people are reading this saying I pray every day but my prayers do not get answers. Why God does not answer my prayers? Did you know that some things only come through praying and fasting? In Mark 9: 26-29, 26 and the spirit cried, and rent him sore, and came out of him: and he was as one dead; insomuch that many said, He is dead. 27 But Jesus took him by the hand, and lifted him up, and he arose. 28 And when he was come into the house, his disciples asked him privately, Why could not we cast him out? 29 And he said unto them, this kind can come forth by nothing, but by prayer and fasting.

In these scriptures, Jesus Disciples failed to cast out a dumb demon in a man's son, but the disciples ask Jesus why? Jesus tells them that some things only come through prayer and fasting. In Matthew 4:2 "And when he had fasted forty days and forty nights, he was afterward a hungered." Jesus Christ fast for 40 days and 40 nights without anything to eat or drink!

Woman Of God: Who Did God Create You to Be?

Men and woman of God certain things only come through fasting and prayer. Many people say I can't fast for 40 days or nights.

In Esther 4:16 "Go, gather together all the Jews that are present in Shushan, and fast ye for me, and neither eat nor drink three days, night or day: I also and my maidens will fast likewise; and so will I go in unto the king, which is not according to the law: and if I perish, I perish." Do not forget Queen Esther fast for 3 days and 3 nights without anything to eat or drink. Queen Esther saved a whole nation from getting destroyed through prayer and fasting. She did not do it alone; she had the whole nation to fast with her. In Matthew 18:19 "Again I say unto you, That if two of you shall agree on earth as touching anything that they shall ask, it shall be done for them of my Father which is in heaven." God said all you need is two and it is already done.

Women and Men of God do not go without anything to eat or drink for more than a day because you will end up dying from hunger and thirst. However, I know you all are thinking you just said fast means to go without eating foods or drinking liquids. Yes you can do that but you must drink water, water is very important. It is very unhealthy to go without food for more than a day.

There are others ways you can fast that are more healthy ways for you and I will show you the proper ways to fast without being hunger or thirsty. When I fast, I do not eat meats and sweets for 21 days. Sometimes I will not watch television; I will not talk on the phone. I will turn my phone off for that whole day or 3 days. Therefore, I will also stay off social websites like Facebook, Instagram, Twitter, Skype and etc. for 21 days also. You can also fast without eating or drinking at certain times like for example at 6pm to 6am I will go without eating during that time but I will drink plenty of water!

There are many different ways you can fast without hurting or damaging your body. Whatever you feel like you need to spend time away from or you feel like it's taking too much of your time away from God, stay away from it for a couple of days. While you're fasting, always remember to pray too because certain things only come through fasting and praying. Therefore, keep praying and fasting until you see results but start making prayer and fasting a part of your daily lives!

What is Your Purpose?

When God created us before we were in our mother's womb, He already had a purpose for our lives. It is a reason why we are born into this world. People always wonder why we are in this world, but God has a reason for everything.

The problem is that the purpose is already inside of us, but it's up to us to find and fulfill our purpose. It saddens me because some people leave this world without fulfilling their purpose for God. It takes a lot of hard work and dedication. Majorly of people living in today's society are too lazy or too scared to do the work or take risks. They rely on others to do the work for them and just want the easy way out. The world does not work like that like.

In Deut 28:13 "The Lord will make you the head and not the tail, and you will always end up at the top and not at the bottom if you obey his commandments which I am urging you today to be careful to do!" If God said He will make you the head and not the tail, why do so many Christians struggle and live below minus wages?

To answer this question truly is because they lack faith, faith Move Mountains and without faith you have nothing. Another reason is because they are so stuck in traditional and religious; therefore, many Christians believe if they go to church and read their bible that's all they have to do. People you will not prosper and multiply if you put a limit on what God can do.

However, it's not all your fault you're only doing what you know and what your parents taught you to do. Therefore, you are who you surround yourself around, stop surrounding yourself around people who lack faith. In this season, you need to be with people on your level with God and people who are higher than you are with God. If you do that, you will change the way you think and you will start thinking like God instead of the world. In fact, you will fail and never prosper if you think the way the world thinks. People get out of religious, traditions, spend time with positive like mind people and start thinking like God instead of the world. The world will fail you but God never will never leave you nor forsake you.

When you start fulfilling your true purpose for God, people will see the God in you and they will know you are the one whom The Lord has blessed.

We Have Failed as Women in Society

They teach us to be strong independent women but they don't teach us how to be wives. So how do we learn to be wives, we learn from the hood. We learn how to live from the system and to rely on the government for what they call financial assistance. We learn how to be single mothers, how to get a man and keep him satisfied. We are never taught how to keep a man. We are never taught how to become wives but to become mothers at a young age. We are taught how to dress hood and half naked to get attention from men.

We are taught how to take someone else man, we are taught how to have multiple baby daddies but we are never taught how a woman suppose to act with class so she can attract a God fearing husband. As a result, we learn what the word hurt means and feels like at a young age. We learn not to depend on men but we can make it on our own. All men do is lie and cheat. All men are dogs and all they want is sex. They don't want to commit, they used you for sex and leave you with a baby.

But in reality, we do need a man in our lives, not just a man but a husband and a provider. Our generation has failed as women talking about we don't need a man.

Stop lying to yourself because we all need a Godly husband because he is your other half. He is what keeps us balanced, in order; he is strong where we are weak. In Genesis 2:18 "And the LORD God said, It is not good that the man should be alone; I will make him a help meet for him."

Woman Of God: Who Did God Create You to Be?

From somewhere down the line, women have lost their ways. We want to be independent so bad but stop being so independent that you refuse to allow a man to come into your world. Stop trying to take roles of the man and be a woman. God created you to be a woman and not a man.

But it's never too late for us women, we can still learn to be wives but not from women who have miserable lives, they teach that mess because they want you unhappy and lonely with them. You might not have a positive role model of a woman in your life but what you do have is that Holy bible that you never take time to read to learn how to become a wife. Don't give up on love, stop listening to all those negative voices and learn how to listen to the voice of the Holy Spirit.

My mother died when I was eight years old so my father raised me. Everything I know now is because I learned it from the word of God.

Stop settling for low life men; learn how to be the proverb 31 woman and your husband will find you. Stop watching reality TV, stop trying to be like those women, be you and stand out from everyone else. God created you to stand out from everyone else and not to be like everybody else. Become the woman God created you to be so you can be a leading example for other women in society.

It's time out for all that mess, the generation curse is broken. I bind that spirit in the name of Jesus. From this forward woman of God stop saying you don't need a man because you do need one. Who else is going to raise your son up to become that Godly man that God created him to be. As women in society, we can only do so much on our own so allow that man to be the husband in your life. Stop rejecting that man that keeps asking you out on a date, the man who is always nice to you at work or the guy who is always nice to you at the market place that always give you extra attention. Woman of God open your eyes up to the word of God so you will know that man when you see him. Stop doubting all men and putting them down, build them up to help them to become stronger so they can find their purpose in life. They already deal with enough rejection from society so don't reject them more.

Learn how to be submissive wives instead of independent women. Trust me we all need a husband, I'm not married yet but trust me whenever God sends me my husband one day I will be ready for him.

In fact, you have to learn how to be a wife first before you can actually become one. However, this is my last and final warning we will no longer fail as women in society! We will no longer come last because God said who was last will become first. In Matthew 20:16 "So the last shall be first, and the first last: for many are called, but few chosen."

Woman of God

    You are loved; stop looking for love in all the wrong places. How can you love someone when you don't even love yourself? God is the only person you should be seeking after. A woman that is after God's heart is a woman cover by God. It doesn't matter what the world thinks or say, you should be after God's heart. You will never find true love until you learn to love yourself. All this time you were looking for someone to love you when God loved you all along!

    I know sometimes it gets hard and you're searching for that Godly husband. When you stop looking that is when your husband will come, your husband should be sent by God. Woman of God wait on God's timing because His timing is so much better than ours. He knows what's best for us. Ester prepared herself a whole year before marrying her King. Woman of God prepare yourselves for your Kings, make sure you're well-groomed, fashionable dress, and smell good.

    In the meantime, while you're waiting on your husband keep your focus on God, He has so much more He wants to offer you. It's a season of everything so in your season of singleness focus on your purpose for God and fulfill His purpose for your life. When Our Lord created us, He created all of us in His very own image so you should never settle for anyone. No matter how lonely you may get, you should never settle. God paid the price for our bodies so treat your body like a temple. In 1 Corinthians 6:19-20 "Or do you not know that your body is a temple of the Holy Spirit within you, whom you have from God? You are not your own, for you were bought with a price. So glorify God in your body."

Woman Of God: Who Did God Create You to Be?

In your time of singleness, keep your focus on God. Whenever I feel lonely, I will spend hours with God, reading my bible, talking to Him, writing and telling Him how I feel. When I do that, I am filled with so much joy and peace. I notice I will be happier and I have peace about it. I trust God timing and I know He knows what's best for me. I don't know about you but I want God's best!

Woman Of God: Who Did God Create You to Be?

About The Author

Christy Sanderson is the Founder of Glory Nation, Author of "Woman of God: Who Did God Create You To Be," "From Nothing into the Woman of God: Spiritual Life," "Woman of God Stop Looking for Love" and an Entrepreneur. She has been featured and on the cover of UBAWA Magazine. Christy has been on several radio interviews: in fact she was even a Co Host on the Digital Breeze radio show in Atlanta, Georgia. Christy is from a small town in Mississippi. Now she lives in Atlanta, Georgia with her son. All Christy's life, writing was her passion to escape her problems. At the young age of 23 Christy fully committed herself to God, let Him take total control of her life and started her own ministry Glory Nation. Her life purpose is to fill God's Glory, to fulfill God's promises to help others become closer to Jesus Christ to find their life purpose.

Woman Of God: Who Did God Create You to Be?

To find out more about Christy's personal ministry, visit www.glorynation.org and follow on social media on Instagram and Periscope @gracefulprincess! Like Facebook page Glory Nation!

Write a review on Amazon & Tag Welcome to the #GloryNation on this #GlorytoGlory #GloryRam on all social media!!!

Be on the lookout for Woman of God Stop Looking for Love part 2!!!

Made in the USA
Middletown, DE
28 December 2022